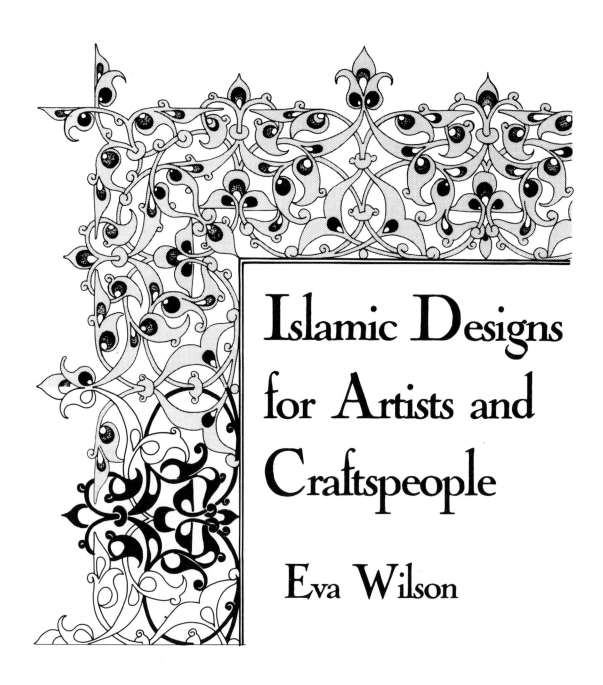

Islamic Designs for Artists and Craftspeople

Eva Wilson

DOVER PUBLICATIONS, INC., New York

Acknowledgement

I am most grateful to the staff of the Department of Oriental Antiquities in the British Museum for making available material for my illustrations and for the use of their library. I particularly thank Rachel Ward for her patience and valuable advice. I have also received help from staff at the Victoria and Albert Museum for which I wish to express my thanks. I am much indebted to Dr James Allen of the Ashmolean Museum, Oxford, for his help and encouragement.

Published in Canada by General Publishing Company, Ltd., 30 Lesmill Road, Don Mills, Toronto, Ontario.

This Dover edition, first published in 1988, is an unabridged republication of the work originally published as a volume in the "British Museum Pattern Books" series by British Museum Publications Ltd, London, in 1988 under the title *Islamic Designs*. The present edition is published by special arrangement with British Museum Publications Ltd, 46 Bloomsbury Street, London WC1B 3QQ.

DOVER *Pictorial Archive* SERIES

Manufactured in the United States of America
Dover Publications, Inc., 31 East 2nd Street, Mineola, N.Y. 11501

Library of Congress Cataloging-in-Publication Data

Wilson, Eva., 1925–
    Islamic designs for artists and craftspeople.

    (Dover pictorial archive series)
    Bibliography: p.
    1. Decoration and ornament, Islamic—Themes, motives.   I. Title.
NK1270.W55   1988   745.4'4917671   88-20237
ISBN 0-486-25819-X (pbk.)

Contents

The World of
Islam

Sites and areas mentioned
in the text.

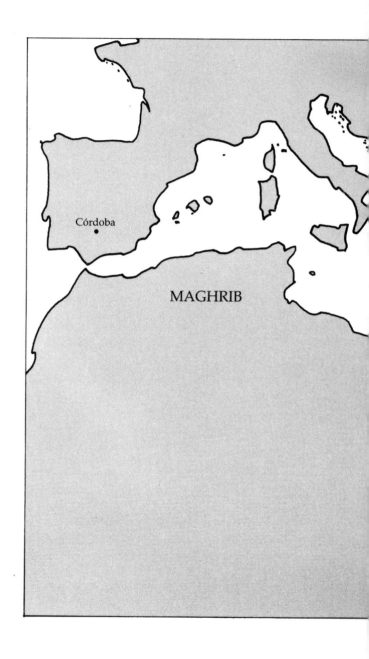

Córdoba

MAGHRIB

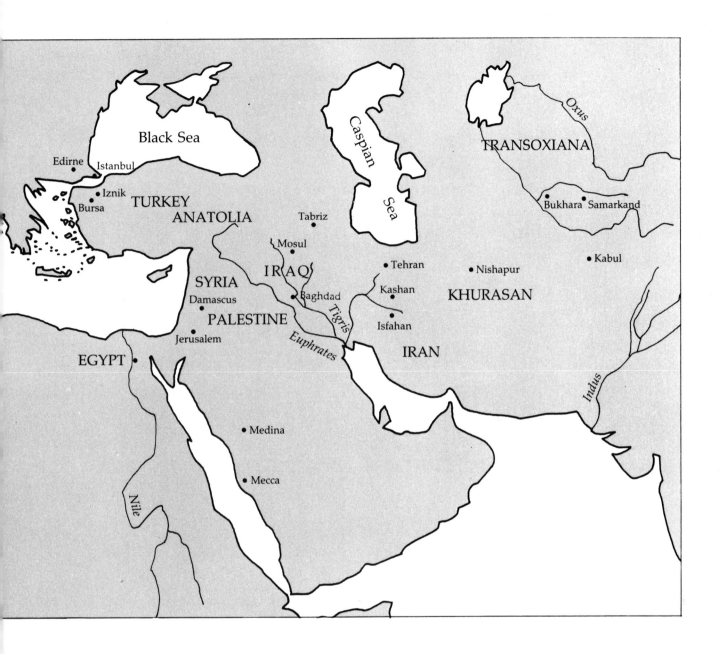

Introduction

The law of the Koran is social as well as spiritual: no aspect of life is untouched by it and therefore all art has to abide by its principles. The complete ban on representational art in the most important contexts, such as in mosques or in the writing and illumination of Korans, is particularly striking and meant that the artistic genius of the Islamic world took a different direction to Christian art.

Islam arose from a desert environment of nomadic people who travelled light—textiles, clothes, carpets and tents were the principal vehicles for visual art and their techniques imposed strict discipline and restricted the range of decorative possibilities. The attitude to art laid down in the Koran reflects this. While Islamic art expanded into other media it remained very disciplined with little interest in individual artistic creativity: the individual artist was expected to work to an exacting standard within established frameworks of designs and techniques.

Designs were passed down from the centres of temporal and spiritual power, (where creativity was directed towards producing buildings in which to worship and towards the interior design of mosques and palaces) and spread through the various crafts, from master to apprentices and to the people who made the humble pots, pans and cloths for everyday use.

The same designs are found throughout the media—designs which originated in book illuminations are also found in carving, metalwork and pottery. They were adapted to different purposes with no regard to scale; even in the most important art, calligraphy, letter forms were scaled up from small books to decorate the domes of mosques.

In selecting the designs for this book it became obvious that only a small part of the available material could be included. I make no attempt to include architecture, or textiles and carpets, although they represent some of the most important groups of material for the understanding of Islamic art, as the necessary technical explanations are beyond the scope of this study (see 'Further reading', p. 23). However, designs inspired by textiles occur frequently in these pages. The designs have also been chosen from a limited geographical area: the Islamic art of Spain, North Africa and India are almost entirely unrepresented, and there are no examples dated later than about 1600. My aim has been to whet the reader's appetite for further exploration of the world of Islamic art by showing some easy examples of complex geometric systems; imaginative uses of simple leaf scrolls; or the fascinating tensions achieved by combining geometrical shapes with flowing scrolls, often using as an intermediary an interlacing element which shares something of the character of both.

Most of the examples illustrated here have been taken from three groups of objects: the illuminated Koran, metalwork and pottery. Designs for the illumination of the Koran undoubtedly met with the approval of the most discerning critics of the day and exemplify the most perfect expressions of the taste of the time. Very little metalwork has been preserved, partly because it was the custom to scrap and re-use metal when objects were broken, worn or no longer fashionable; there is, however, some very fine metalwork available for study. Lavishly-decorated metal vessels belonged to rich and powerful people, who demanded a high standard of workmanship and design. Pottery could be very sophisticated, though for much of the Muslim world the best was Chinese porcelain; local pottery was used by those who could not afford the best. Pottery, however, allows for a more individualistic treatment of decoration, and many of the most attractive designs are taken from this body of material.

The designs are arranged not geographically or chronologically but by related motifs and design systems. **1–7** illustrate the decorative use of calligraphy (see also p. 11) and some representational designs of animals and men are shown **8–17**. Geometric designs are discussed p. 14 and illustrated **18–49**. Examples of ribbon interlace, sometimes combined with plant ornament and leaf scrolls are illustrated **50–67**, while the designs from **68** onwards are plant ornaments, mainly variations on the palmette and the arabesque, but also including examples of Chinese lotus and other oriental motifs as well as some floral designs from pottery and tiles produced at Iznik in Turkey in the Ottoman period.

Brief outline of the history of the Islamic empire

The vast distances between the capitals of the empire meant that it could only be held together by strong rulers, and in their absence it fragmented, leaving the way free for new dynasties to take their place. These dynasties founded new capitals in different parts of the empire where their courts would attract skilled local craftsmen along with those whose services were no longer needed in the old, abandoned capital towns of a conquered dynasty. This was one reason why strong similarities are found in Islamic art from widely-separated parts of the empire.

After the death of Muhammad in 632 his followers came out of Arabia to conquer Syria and Egypt (then part of the Byzantine empire), and won Iran and Iraq, putting an end to the Sasanian rulers and inflicting many blows from which other mighty though enfeebled powers never recovered. By the early eighth century North Africa and Spain also became a part of Islam along with areas to the east in Transoxiana and the Indus Valley.

To control such an empire the Caliphs of the Omayyad dynasty needed a more central capital than Medina and so they established themselves in Damascus.

When the Omayyad dynasty was overthrown by the Abbasids in 750 Baghdad was made the capital. A member of the Omayyad family did however establish himself as an independent ruler in Spain with a capital at Córdoba, where his successors ruled until the middle of the eleventh century. Egypt also became independent under the Fatimid dynasty which founded Cairo in 969. Local dynasties in the east created their own capitals at Nishapur and Bukhara.

In the eleventh century a Turkish tribe from Central Asia, the Seljuqs, conquered the whole Islamic world as far as Syria, and extended it to include most of Asia Minor. It was only in the second half of the twelfth century that Syria and Egypt were united under the Egyptian dynasties of the Ayyubids (1176–1250) and the Mamluks (1250–1517).

By far the greatest upheaval was caused by the Mongol invasion from Central Asia which began with the brutal devastation of Khurasan in 1220 and was completed by the sack of Baghdad in 1258. The resistance by the Seljuqs of Asia Minor to Mongol attacks came to an end in the thirteenth century. They were succeeded by another Turkish family, the Ottomans, in the middle of the fourteenth century. In 1453 Constantinople became their capital and the Ottoman empire survived to 1924. Egypt, having escaped the Mongol invasions, was at last conquered by the Ottomans in 1517.

The Mongol dynasty of the Il-Khanids in Persia and its successors lasted until the end of the fourteenth century when the Mongols again invaded from the east under Timur (Tamerlane), whose dynasty was in turn superseded by the Safavids who ruled Iran until the eighteenth century.

This succession of events influenced the art of Islam in various ways. The conquered areas consolidated their own strong artistic traditions: particularly the classical tradition of the Byzantine empire and the Central Asian and Iranian traditions of the Sasanian empire. The emergence of rich, powerful courts encouraged all types of arts and crafts; the growth of towns and cities through trade, manufacture and administration created new markets and exposed local craftsmen to the arts of other lands and imported goods, particularly porcelain from China, exerted a strong influence on style and ornament.

More powerful still was the unifying influence of Islam itself. This was expressed particularly through the Arabic language and the script in which it was written. The followers of Muhammad brought no particular art style out of Arabia, only the script, which was regarded as an expression both of art and of religion, and ideas about art and its purpose.

The Koran, calligraphy and illumination

Arabic script evolved very late compared with other systems of writing, some of which go back thousands of years. The Arabs of the pre-Islamic period relied largely on oral tradition, especially for poetry for which they had a passionate interest. The Koran was first transmitted by word of mouth. However, it soon became necessary to set it down in writing, and the Arabic script then rapidly developed into an astonishingly beautiful artistic medium.

Arabic belongs to a group of Semitic scripts, most closely related to the script of the Nabataeans, a semi-nomadic people who lived between Sinai and southern Syria in the first century AD and this script was in turn derived from the Aramaic. Arabic script developed in the fifth and sixth centuries, local forms and variations gradually merging into an approved script for all the Arabs. With the advent of Islam it assumed a sacred status for it was the script especially chosen by God to transmit his message to all men. The need to record the Koran, and to create a worthy vehicle for the message, played a central role in the development of the script and led to a preoccupation with clarity and legibility as well as with the beauty of the script. At this point it ceases to be mere script and becomes calligraphy, produced by trained artist scribes.

The first copies of the Koran were probably produced in the middle of the seventh century. By the eighth century the Kufic form of the script emerged as the most important of several variants. It is fairly austere with a low vertical profile and a horizontal emphasis, typically written on oblong or extended rectangular pages and panels.

The Arabic alphabet includes the consonants and three long vowels–a, i and u. At a time when Islam was spreading rapidly among non-Arabs, it was necessary to make it easier to learn Arabic, in order to read the Koran, and to become assimilated into the Muslin community. To standardise the text a system of dots and marks were added to the Kufic script which differentiated between letters of similar form and indicated vowels to aid correct pronunciation.

Inscriptions in Kufic were also treated decoratively on textiles, carving, metalwork, glass and pottery. Here the uprights might be plaited or embellished with terminals of leaves or even human heads (1–5). The text often appears against a background of scrolls as part of a decorative scheme or reduced to a geometric design barely distinguishable as a script (5 BOTTOM, 76 BOTTOM). Texts on domestic or secular objects often simply give the name of Allah or the word *blessing*, but quotations from the Koran are also common. Very occasionally they feature the name of the maker or, more often, of the patron who commissioned the object (1–8).

Cursive calligraphy developed from carved and rounded early scripts used for secular purposes. Several important forms of cursive script developed in the Omayyad period (661–750) with the increased volume of writing generated by the administration of the expanding empire. By the early decades of the Abbasid period these became more numerous until there were over twenty cursive styles in common use by the late ninth century. It was at this point that an accomplished Baghdad calligrapher, Abu ʿAli Muhammad ibn Muqla, created a system which laid down the ideal proportions of individual letters. The system was based on the width of the nib of the reed pen: a rhomboid dot was made by pressing the pen diagonally on the paper, the length of the dot's parallel sides being the width of the pen's nib (◆). A particular number of these dots (which varied with the style of script) set point to point determined the height of the letter *Alif*, written as a straight vertical stroke. A circle with the diameter of the *Alif's* length completed the standards of proportion on the basis of which all other letters of the alphabet were drawn.

The number of cursive scripts based on this system was restricted to six, of which only one is illustrated here. This is Thuluth, which was the script most often used for decorative purposes (6–7). **79** shows a Thuluth inscription superimposed on the decorative frontispiece of a Koran produced in Cairo in 1304 by one of the great Mamluk calligraphers.

The theorists of Muslim art were opposed to figurative representation in religious contexts and such representations are on the whole rare anywhere in Islamic art. Originally the Koran was not illuminated at all, but it was soon felt necessary to mark the beginning of a book, a chapter or a verse. This initially took the form of modest panels at the beginning of a book, palmette designs in the margin at the beginning of a chapter and small rosettes between verses. The designs on pls. **70–71** are taken from a Koran written in the year 1000 in Baghdad. The repertoire of motifs reflects the mixture of traditions and styles available to the artist at the centre of the Islamic world at that time: lotus designs from China and Egypt, scrolls of split palmettes, palmette flowers and rosettes from the Mediterranean classical tradition; and the winged, beaded and feathered designs of the Sasanian tradition from Central Asia and Iran. These decorations subsequently became more lavish; frontispieces covered entire pages with intricate geometrical designs, the spaces filled with leaf scrolls, the interlaced borders decorated in gold, blue and red (**30, 35, 48–55, 56** TOP, **57** TOP, **66–7, 76, 78–81**).

The early Korans were written on parchment (prepared skins of goat and sheep), vellum (calf skins) or, mainly in Egypt, on papyrus. Later paper was used; this had to be imported from China until the secret of its manufacture was revealed to the Arabs, allegedly after the defeat of the Chinese at the battle of Samarkand in 750. The paper was a pure rag paper made from linen fibres.

Pens were made of sharpened reeds and brushes from squirrel, buffalo, camel or cat hair set in feather quills.

Lamp black mixed with soot and gum arabic (a sticky secretion from certain types of acacia tree) was used for sketching; waterproof ink was made from vitriol (sulphate of iron) and gall nuts. Pigments were mostly mineral: for instance, cinnabar and sulphide of mercury for reds, lapis lazuli and azurite for blue, malachite for green and shades of ochre for yellow, brown and reds. White was produced from chalk or lead carbonite. Some organic pigments were also used such as forms of cochineal and indigo. All pigments were mixed with a gum arabic medium. Gold was applied as gold leaf or as a crushed metal mixed with animal size.

Pottery

Islam brought important developments in manufacture and trade to the towns of the Middle East. Imported white porcelain from T'ang China in the ninth century inspired local potters to produce a ware of similar appearance. The materials and technology which made Chinese porcelain uniquely hard and white were not available here. However, local potters could draw on a long tradition of glazing pottery, although all were low-fired earthenware (fired at 1000–1200°C); these included both alkaline glazes, often with added tin oxides which produced an opaque white colour, and lead glazes. Two techniques were developed in the ninth century: in one the white surface was produced by a lead glaze made opaque and white by the addition of small amounts of tin oxide (or other opacifier), and in the other a white slip covered the coloured earthenware body under a clear lead glaze.

The tin-glazed techniques began to be used in the western and central parts of the Islamic world, particularly in Egypt and Iraq. Initially it may have been used to produce cheap copies of Chinese ware, but soon characteristically Islamic designs were developed, painted in blue on the glaze before firing (3 TOP).

The distinctive lustre effect which is particularly associated with Islamic pottery from the ninth to the fourteenth centuries was developed from a technique probably borrowed from the decoration of glass. It was a complicated technique and became a closely-guarded secret among the potters who practised the art. First the undecorated pot was glazed and fired. The design was painted on the cold glaze surface with a mixture of sulphur, silver and copper oxides which was combined with an earth medium such as ochre and suspended in vinegar. The pot was then fired a second time, at a lower temperature (to prevent the glaze melting and running), and in a reducing atmosphere, that is with a restricted air supply. The oxygen in the metal oxides was extracted from the paint when it combined with carbon monoxide to form carbon dioxide. After firing the ochre would be rubbed off to reveal the design in a variety of metallic colours from gold to red and brown depending on the relative proportions of the metal oxides used. The paint was easy to apply to the glazed surface and fine and intricate designs were achieved (8 BOTTOM, 9 TOP, 12–15, 68–9).

The ancient technique of applying a thin layer of white clay as a liquid slip to the still wet earthenware body of a pot was later developed further, particularly in Iran. Designs were painted in slips of different colours—usually black, brown or red—on the white foundation and covered with a clear glaze fluxed with lead oxide (1–3, 4 TOP, 8 TOP). Designs were also incised or carved through the white slip to allow the coloured clay of the body to show through (9 BOTTOM, 25). The lead glaze could be stained with iron, copper or manganese to produce shades of yellow, green or purple; these colours did not, however, mix in the free-flowing glaze and usually appear as splashes or streaks of colour.

A new material, an artificial frit body, was developed in Egypt in the twelfth century and spread rapidly to all other pottery-making areas in Syria and Iran. It consisted mainly of finely-ground quartz bound with plastic white clay and a little glaze mixture; it was white throughout. Thin vessels produced in this ware initially imitated a new style of translucent porcelain imported from China, but it also allowed Muslim potters to produce a large range of pottery in techniques and styles unrelated to Chinese wares. These include lustre ware of exceptional quality (14–15), designs in black slip under a clear glaze (10 CENTRE, 73) and over-glaze painting in many colours (77 TOP).

Most important, however, was the invention in Kashan, Iran, in about 1200 of an alkaline glaze (fluxed with potassium oxide in the form of plant ash) which allowed fine painting to be carried out directly on the surface of the frit body and covered with a transparent glaze without the colours spreading into the glaze during firing (74–75). This technique, combined with the use of cobalt blue, was adopted by the Chinese in the fourteenth century and was the basis of their blue and white porcelains. From this time onward, the overwhelming influence on Islamic pottery was the popularity of Chinese blue and white wares which were now imported in very large quantities. However, as before, the Muslim potters showed a good deal of independence in their decoration. The blue and white hexagonal tiles of the mid-fifteenth century in the Mosque of Murad II at Edirne, the capital of the Ottoman empire prior to the conquest of Istanbul, feature a mixture of Islamic designs and designs of Chinese inspiration set together, apparently at random, in a decorative panel with triangular turquoise spacer tiles (36).

When the court moved to the new capital in Istanbul in 1453, it is likely that the local potters who produced the tiles at Edirne moved to Iznik where the imperial kilns were established. A tradition of pottery-making already existed at Iznik, where supplies of white clay and sand (as well as the availability of wood, water and minerals) made it an ideal site for the vastly-increased production of pottery and tiles generated by an extensive building program in the capital.

During the reign of Süleyman the Magnificent (1520–1566) all forms of Ottoman art and culture flourished. Styles and decorations on cloth, ceramics, metalwork or in wood carving were strongly influenced by designs originally created for book illustrations, reaffirming the pre-eminence of this art form in the Islamic world. Three styles can be distinguished as particularly typical of the decorative art of this period, illustrated here mainly by examples taken from pottery and tiles. First, the re-interpretation of the traditional leaf and floral scrolls (**86, 95–7**). Second, the *saz* style, a composite style derived from drawings of an 'enchanted forest' and adapted to scroll designs with additional long serrated *saz* leaves and fantastic flowers to produce a restless, twisting and turning effect (**87, 89**) and third, a naturalistic style of garden flowers and trees in balanced, natural sprays (**90–1**). However, *saz* and naturalistic motifs are often present on the same object, each tempering the effect of the other (**93**).

The ceramic products at Iznik until its decline in the seventeenth century (whether pottery or tiles) were of an extremely high quality, the hard white body coated with a fine slip and the design painted in clear brilliant colours of blue, green, purple, black and a strong red applied as a slip.

Metalwork

It is striking that even among the best of surviving Islamic metalwork, few vessels are made entirely of silver or gold. Muslim metalworkers, however, created superb objects of bronze or brass inlaid with copper, silver and gold. Metalworkers enjoyed a high social status, and it is obvious from the designs on vessels such as the ewer made in Mosul in 1232, from which I have taken many designs (**16–17, 39** CENTRE, **40, 41** TOP, **56** BOTTOM), that the very best artists were involved in their manufacture. It is also apparent that the designer of the medallions on this ewer (**16–17**) was an artist who primarily specialised in book illustration. There are many links between designs on metal and the art of the book (**56–9**). In turn it would appear that pottery often imitated designs on metal (**24–5, 60–1**).

The alloys used for most of the metalwork cannot always be determined and the terms brass or bronze are frequently used indiscriminately. Casting was by the lost wax process or by moulding in sand, but vessels were also raised from sheet metal. Decoration was carried out by graving, chasing and by different forms of inlay and repoussé, where the ornament is raised in relief from the reverse side, or by a combination of these methods.

Geometrical designs

In ancient Mesopotamia, as in ancient Egypt, simple geometry was used in measurement of land, in construction of buildings and in astronomical calculations. The Greeks developed this knowledge: Euclid included all known geometry in the first systematic treatise of the subject written around 300 BC in the mathematical school in Alexandria. The manuscripts containing this knowledge were dispersed widely and became available to the Arab world by the end of the eighth century.

Geometry became highly important in the Islamic world as its figures and constructions were permeated with symbolic, cosmological and philosophical significance. In architecture strict adherence to geometric principles in plans and elevations was the basis of the harmony and discipline which characterise all Islamic art. In decoration geometrically-based designs covered entire surfaces, typically with a geometrical framework leaving spaces to be filled with interlaced and stylised leaf and floral designs (**30, 35, 48, 66, 79–81**).

The close association between geometry, cosmology and symbolism has led some scholars (for instance Keith Critchlow, *Islamic Patterns. An Analytical and*

Cosmological Approach, 1976) to read metaphysical and religious significance into the geometrical content of both finished designs and the postulated grids on which the designs must have been based. This aspect of geometrical design will not be discussed here. While it is probable that geometrical designs were not seen merely as abstract patterns but as imbued with a sacred content (particularly in religious contexts), it seems unlikely that the craftsman decorating a wall or carving a door would have had these properties uppermost in his mind. Rather he would be following the teaching of his master and the traditional skills of his craft, and he would no doubt have left to others the philosophical interpretations of the traditional patterns he produced.

There appears to be no evidence of the kind of grids and construction systems which must have been used to plan and execute these designs, and a variety of different systems have been postulated. The constructions in the so-called 'pattern book' of the 19th-century Persian decorator Mirza Akbar in the Victoria and Albert Museum have not been sufficiently analysed to allow any conclusions to be drawn from these simple sketches. I make no attempt here to put forward another hypothetical system, nor to go too deeply into the intricacies of these problems. Nevertheless, geometrical designs have to be based on a grid system. Issam El-Said and Ayşe Parman in *Geometric concepts in Islamic art* (1976) put forward a system in which geometrical grids are broken down into identical units which are repeated in regular sequence. This is a practical and useful method of constructing geometrical patterns. One of its advantages is that the number of identical units in the area to be decorated can be determined by first dividing the area into, for instance, squares or hexagons of equal size. Within each of these is inscribed a geometrical figure which serves as a basis for a grid on which the pattern of the unit is drawn. Each unit links up on all sides with other identical units to form the design. Another advantage of the system is that designs can be enlarged or reduced on the basis of the proportional relationships between geometrical figures. Examples of some basic constructions and repeat units, and a few designs based on these, are illustrated **26–49**.

Geometrical designs are basically very simple: they may be constructed with only a compass and a rule and the knowledge of certain procedures which produce triangles, squares, hexagons, stars, etc. The designs may be reduced and enlarged with great ease. By repeating these procedures, and through further division and the addition of straight and curved lines, almost limitless elaborate variations may be achieved. Once the grid has been laid down there is scope for individual experimentation. Although these designs often appear highly complex there are no mysteries; all that is needed is a logical approach and a steady hand and nerve. The best way to understand the geometrical patterns is to draw them. (For further examples of this type of design see El-Said and Parman, 1976, mentioned above, and the reprint of J. Bourgoin's plates from *Les Eléments de l'art Arabe: le trait des entrelacs*, originally published in Paris 1879; in Dover Pictorial Archive Series 1973 under the title *Arabic geometrical pattern and design*).

The leaf scroll motif

One motif—the leaf scroll—occurs more often than any other in these pages and in all its various forms it owes nothing to living plants. Its origin lies in ancient Egypt where the simple formula of two curving petals flanking a central lobe became the foundation for one of the world's most popular and enduring motifs, the palmette. When cut in half and attached to a spiralling or undulating scroll (a device which can also be tracked back to Egypt and Mycenae), it becomes a most versatile decorative motif (**62–3, 66–73, 76–83**). Together with the plaited and interlaced borders, frames and knots (**50–7**) and key patterns (**40–1**), which are also motifs of ancient ancestry and enduring popularity, the palmette flower and scroll are among the handful of decorative devices which seem never to go out of fashion. Many textile and wallpaper designs today feature one or other of these motifs.

We have seen that the Mediterranean influence was one of the elements which determined the character of Islamic art. Other influences came from the east; first, the non-figurative and stylised art of Central Asia and, later, with the Mongol invasions and strong trade links with China, many floral motifs were added to the repertoire of the Muslim artist. Islam's own unique contribution lay primarily in calligraphy and architecture and in the particular use of geometric designs, as well as in the spiritual and philosophical attitude to the art.

The Muslim craftsman produced stunning results on the basis of simple geometric principles and traditional motifs, beautifully carried out. At times they may be limited more by the constraints of the artist's vision and beliefs than those of the medium. For the designer/craftsman the most striking feature of Islamic decoration is the competence and flair with which it is executed.

Notes on the Designs

1 Painted design on earthenware bowl. White slip with brown decoration under a clear lead glaze. Diameter 21.8 cm. Eastern Iran, 10th century. *Freer Gallery of Art*, Washington DC (56.1).

2 Earthenware bowls with designs painted in black or brown slips on a white ground under a clear lead glaze. Eastern Iran, 9th–10th centuries. TOP LEFT Diameter 23.75 cm. *Metropolitan Museum of Art*, New York (38.40.142), RIGHT Diameter 32 cm. *Private collection*. BOTTOM Diameter 35.5 cm. *Iran Bastan Museum*, Teheran (8378).

3 White tin-glazed earthenware bowls with designs painted in cobalt blue. Iraq, 9th–10th centuries. LEFT Diameter 20 cm. *Private collection*, RIGHT Diameter 20.3 cm. *Metropolitan Museum of Art*, New York (63.159.4). BOTTOM Painted design on an earthenware bowl. Black and red slips (indicated here by a screen) on a cream ground under a clear lead glaze. Diameter 21.6 cm. Nishapur, Iran, 9th–10th centuries. *British Museum*, London (1967 12–13.1).

4 TOP Earthenware plate painted in dark brown slip on a white ground under a clear lead glaze. Diameter 46.8 cm. Iran, 10th century. *Freer Gallery of Art*, Washington DC (52.11). BOTTOM LEFT Detail from a band of ornamental Kufic script on the shoulder of a brass ewer inlaid with copper and silver. Khurasan, Iran, late 12th or early 13th centuries. *British Museum*, London (48 8–5.2); RIGHT *In the name of God the merciful* carved in Kufic script on a marble tombstone. Length 75 cm. Egypt, 9th–10th centuries. *British Museum*, London (1975 4–15.1).

5 TOP Decorative Kufic letters, probably reading *glory*, carved in low relief on a plate under a clear glaze. Diameter 30.6 cm. Northwestern Iran, 12th century. *Metropolitan Museum of Art*, New York. BOTTOM LEFT Plaited, knotted and foliated Kufic script forming the word *power* carved in wood. Turkey, *c*. 13th century. Illustrated in Y. H. Safadi, *Islamic Calligraphy*, 1978, fig. 126. RIGHT Glazed tile in blue, turquoise and white, said to have come from the Royal Mosque in Isfahan. 35.5 cm square. Early 17th century. *Art Institute of Chicago* (1926.1186).

6 TOP Tile painted underglaze in blue with reserved *Thuluth* script in white reading *Glory to our Master, the Sultan al-Malik al-Ashraf Abu'l-Nasir Qaytbay. May his victory be glorious.* Diameter 29 cm. Egypt, late 15th century. *National Museum*, Kuwait. CENTRE Carved ivory panel. Length 28.2 cm. Egypt 14th century. *Walters Art Gallery*, Baltimore. BOTTOM Marble panel. Length 57.8 cm. Egypt?, first half 13th century. *David Collection*, Copenhagen (33/1986).

7 Openwork door panel of steel. The inscription reads: *It is from Solomon and reads as follows: in the name of God, the merciful, the compassionate, the year 1105 of the Hijra.* 34.3 × 25.4 cm. Probably Isfahan, Iran, 1693–4. *British Museum*, London (OA 368).

8 TOP Earthenware bowls with designs painted in black slip on a white ground under a clear lead glaze. In the bowl LEFT this glaze is tinted yellow. Diameter 18.4 cm. Nishapur, East Iran. RIGHT Diameter 14 cm. East Iran or Transoxiana. *Los Angeles County Museum of Art* (M. 73.5.130 and 129) BOTTOM Design painted in lustre on a tin-glazed earthenware bowl. Diameter 22 cm. Iraq. *Private collection*. 10th century.

9 TOP Designs painted in lustre on tin-glazed earthenware bowls. Iraq, 10th century. LEFT *Metropolitan Museum of Art*, New York (64.259); RIGHT *David Collection*, Copenhagen (44/1967). BOTTOM The design on this earthenware bowl was cut through a white slip to expose the darker clay underneath. The clear lead glaze is tinted a pale green. Diameter 17.7 cm. Iran, 12th century. *Victoria and Albert Museum*, London (C. 285–1927).

10 TOP LEFT Design engraved inside a bronze bowl. Diameter of motif 8.7 cm. 14th–15th centuries. *British Museum*, London (1985 11–20.1). TOP RIGHT and BOTTOM Details of ornaments engraved on a bronze bowl. Diameter of roundel approximately 2 cm, width of border approximately 1.5 cm. Khurasan, Iran, early 13th century. *Victoria and Albert Museum*, London (M. 388–1911). CENTRE Design painted in black slip on a frit ware bowl under a turquoise clear glaze. Diameter 14.5 cm. Iran, 12th century. *Victoria and Albert Museum*, London (C. 82–1918).

11 TOP LEFT Design painted in black slip under a clear glaze on a frit ware bowl. Diameter 20.5 cm. Iran, second half 12th century. *British Museum*, London (1956 7–28.4). TOP RIGHT and CENTRE Designs painted in lustre on tin-glazed earthenware bowls. TOP RIGHT Diameter 19.5 cm. Egypt, 11th century. *Private collection*; CENTRE Diameter 15.5 cm. Syria, second half of 12th century. *Victoria and Albert Museum*, London (C. 50–1952). BOTTOM Detail of the design on the rim of a large metal dish. Width of border approximately 5 cm. Iran, late 12th or early 13th centuries. *British Museum*, London (1967 12–14.1).

12 Designs painted in lustre on tin-glazed bowls. TOP Diameter 35.9 cm. *Freer Gallery of Art*, Washington DC (25.6); BOTTOM Diameter 15 cm. *Victoria and Albert Museum*, London (C. 62–1981). Iraq, 10th century.

13 Designs painted in lustre. TOP Tile. Diameter 13.5 cm. Iran, late 12th century. *Victoria and Albert Museum*, London (C. 444–1911); BOTTOM Diameter 20.5 cm. Syria, 12th century. *David Collection*, Copenhagen (Isl. 195).

14 Design on a large bowl painted in lustre. Diameter 43.2 cm. Iran, late 12th–early 13th centuries. *Freer Gallery of Art*, Washington DC (57.21).

15 Design on a large bowl painted in lustre. Diameter 35.2 cm. Iran, 12th century. *Keir Collection*, London (151).

16–17 Details from a brass ewer. Dated by inscription to 1232 at Mosul, Iraq. *British Museum*, London (1866 12–29.61).

18–19 Keith Critchlow, *Islamic Patterns. An Analytical and Cosmological Approach*, 1976, pp. 16–23.

20 TOP LEFT Design painted in black under a clear blue glaze on a bowl. Diameter 14 cm. Nishapur, Iran, late 12th–early 13th centuries. *Iran Bastan Museum*, Teheran. TOP RIGHT Formalised drawing of the design of a bowl incised through a white slip and covered by a clear glaze tinted in splashes of yellow, green and brown. Diameter 32.4 cm. Nishapur, Iran, 10th century. *British Museum*, London (1956 5–18.1). BOTTOM Plaster panel in low relief. 186.5 × 21.3 cm. Nishapur, Iran, 10th century. *Metropolitan Museum of Art*, New York.

21 Engraved design in the centre of a bronze plate. Iran, 10th–11th centuries. *British Museum*, London (1949 2–17.2).

22 LEFT TOP Design on frit ware bowl painted in black and blue under a clear alkaline glaze. Diameter 21.8 cm. Kashan, Iran, 13th century. BOTTOM Design inside an earthenware bowl incised and painted in brown, yellow and green under a clear lead glaze. Syria, early 14th century. *Ashmolean Museum*, Oxford (1956.119 and 1978.1761). RIGHT detail in blind tooling from a bookbinding. Egypt?, 15th century. *Victoria and Albert Museum*, London (366/6–1888).

23 LEFT The central design engraved on a brass tripod stand. Khurasan?, Iran, early 14th century. *Victoria and Albert Museum*, London (M.823–1928). RIGHT Detail from a metal writing box inlaid with silver and gold. Diameter of detail 4.6 cm. Egypt c. 1300–1350. *British Museum*, London (81 8–2.20).

24 Design engraved inside a shallow brass dish. Diameter of the design 43 cm. Iran, late 12th–early 13th centuries. *British Museum*, London (1967 12–14.1).

25 TOP Diameter 18 cm. Iran, 11th–12th centuries. *Private collection*. BOTTOM, Iran 10th–11th centuries. *Fitzwilliam Museum*, Cambridge (C. 148.1946).

26–29 I. El-Said and A. Parman, *Geometric Concepts in Islamic Art*, 1976, figs 12–15, 27, 35a,b, 36b.

30 Cairo, 15th century. *National Library*, (Koran 98 vol. 1f. 178r).

31 TOP The geometric frameworks of three roundels from a Koran. Spain?, 12th century. *Turkish and Islamic Museum*, Istanbul (360). BELOW Knot motifs painted in coloured slips in the centre of 10th-century earthenware bowls; LEFT diameter of motif approximately 13 cm. Iran. *Freer Gallery of Art*, Washington DC (53.70), CENTRE diameter of motif approximately 4 cm. Nishapur, East Iran. *Metropolitan Museum of Art*, New York (40.170.25), RIGHT diameter of motif approximately 8.5 cm. Nishapur?, East Iran or Transoxiana. *Iran Bastan Museum*, Teheran (3140). BOTTOM Painted border from a Koran. Syria?, 13th century. *Turkish and Islamic Museum*, Istanbul (439).

32–34 I. El-Said and A. Parman, *Geometric Concepts in Islamic Art*, 1976, figs 5a, 38a,b, 41, 42, 47, 49, 77a.

35 Egypt, 1356. *National Library*, Cairo (Koran 8f. 2r).

36 Tiles as in the Mosque of Murad II at Edirne. Hexagonal tiles are 22.5 cm between parallel sides. This combination of patterned tiles is not original but is a representative selection of the designs present and reflects their random distribution. Mid-15th century.

37 Hexagonal tile painted in blue and turquoise (indicated by a screen). Maximum diameter 22.5 cm. Iznik, Turkey, c. 1540. *British Museum*, London (OA 623–4).

38 I. El-Said and A. Parman, *Geometric Concepts in Islamic Art*, 1976, figs 45, 50.

39 TOP Engraved and inlaid roundels on brass caskets. Western Iran, 13th century. *Victoria and Albert Museum*, London (756–1889 and 757–1889). CENTRE One of several roundels engraved and inlaid with the same design on a brass ewer dated by inscription to 1232 at Mosul, Iraq. The roundels typically have a diameter of 1.5–2 cm. BOTTOM Border on the lid of a writing box, engraved and inlaid in silver and gold. Width 1.9 cm. Egypt, c. 1300–1350. *British Museum*, London (1866 12–29.61 and 81 8–2.20).

40 These examples of the very common key patterns are taken from a brass ewer dated 1232 and made at Mosul and an early 14th-century brass casket. *British Museum*, London (1866 12–29.61 and 1957 8–1.1).

41 TOP Roundel from brass ewer made at Mosul in 1232. Such roundels are typically 1.5–2 cm in diameter. *British Museum*, London (1866 12–29.61). BELOW LEFT and CENTRE Roundels from brass bowl. Diameter 0.8–1.3 cm. *Galleria Estense*, Modena (8082); RIGHT roundel from a writing box, Iran 1281. *British Museum*, London (91 6–23.5). BOTTOM Roundel from a bronze dish. Khurasan, Iran, 1496–7. *Victoria and Albert Museum*, London (374–1897).

42 TOP, LEFT Motif from earthenware bowl painted in lustre. Egypt, 10th–11th centuries. *Metropolitan Museum of Art*, New York (1975.32.2); CENTRE openwork grid at the top of a sprinkler in cast bronze. Diameter approximately 4 cm. Khurasan, 10th–11th centuries. *Victoria and Albert Museum*, London (777–1889); RIGHT motif painted in slip under a clear glaze. Diameter of motif 9.5 cm. Transoxiana, 10th century. *Los Angeles County Museum of Art* (M. 73.5.199). BELOW LEFT Design of interlaced ducks (also shown separately on the right) on the lid of a brass box. Approximately 4 × 4 cm. Mosul, Iraq, 1233–59. *British Museum*, London (78 12–30.674); RIGHT Motif from plate painted in brown and red slips under a clear glaze. Diameter of motif 7.5 cm. Iran, 10th century. *Freer Gallery of Art*, Washington DC (65.27). BOTTOM Engraved design in the centre of a brass plate. Diameter 7 cm. Iran, 12th century. *British Museum*, London (1956 7–26.12).

43 The common rotating motif as a single unit TOP and as a repeat unit BELOW after I. El-Said and A. Parman, *Geometric Concepts in Islamic Art*, 1976, fig. 23 are based on the octagon. K. Critchlow in *Islamic Patterns. An Analytical and Cosmological Approach*, 1976, p. 72 illustrates this motif based on the dodecagon and discusses the significance of the geometrical relationships which arise from this method.

44, 45 LEFT, **46, 47** I. El-Said and A. Parman, *Geometric Concepts in Islamic Art*, 1976, 4a–c, 61a,b, 62, 65, 97. **45** RIGHT K. Critchlow, *Islamic Patterns*, 1976, p. 85.

48 The central panel from a Koran frontispiece. 11.6 × 7.6 cm. Egypt, 14th century. *British Library*, London (Or. 848 f. 1v).

49 TOP The framework only in blind tooling on a leather bookbinding. Diameter approximately 5 cm. Turkey, 15th century. *Chester Beatty Library*, Dublin (Moritz collection 9). BOTTOM Detail from Koran frontispiece. Cairo, 1372. *National Library*, Cairo (Koran 10, 2r).

50–51 Interlacing borders from illuminated Korans painted in gold on vellum with some blue and red. **50** First and third borders from the top: width of borders approximately 1 cm. Near East, Iraq or Iran, 9th century. *Nurosmaniye Mosque Library*, Istanbul (27, ff. 154v–155r). Second border from the top: Damascus, 10th century. *Chester Beatty Library*, Dublin (MS 1421 fol. 2a). Fourth and fifth border from the top **50** and **51**: details from a Koran. Egypt?, 10th century. *British Library*, London (Add. 11735).

52–53 Borders with ribbon interlace from illuminated Korans. **52** and the third, fourth and fifth borders from the top of **53**: Cairo, 1304. *British Library*, London (Add. 22407). First border from the top of **53**: Egypt?, 14th century. *Chester Beatty Library*, Dublin (1629); second border, Iran, 15th century. *Mashhad Shrine Library* (416, ff. 1v–2r).

54 Borders with ribbon interlace from illuminated Korans. From the top: First border, Cairo, 1369. *National Library*, Cairo (Koran 7, ff. 1v–2r). Second border, Egypt, 14th century. *Chester Beatty Library*, Dublin (MS 1479 fol. 2a). Third border, Marrakesh, 1202–3. *Topkapi Saray Library*, Istanbul (R33, ff. 68v–69r). Fourth border, Cairo, 1334. *National Library*, Cairo (Koran 81, ff. 375v–376r).

55 The interlaced framework LEFT and RIGHT and the detail of the construction of the interlace TOP are from a Koran produced in Mosul 1310. *British Library*, London (Or. 4945, ff. 1v–2r). The examples inside the framework which show different methods of turning corners in interlace borders are taken LEFT from a

Koran produced in Iran 1430–1. *Pars Museum*, Shiraz (430 MP); RIGHT from a Koran produced in 1424. *Mashad Shrine Library* (414, ff. 1v–2r).

56 TOP LEFT The framework only of an ornamental detail from a Koran, probably produced in Spain. 12th century. *Topkapi Saray Library*, Istanbul (E.H. 40 ff. 107v–108r); RIGHT detail from a bronze casket. Diameter 1.8 cm. Iran, early 14th century. *British Museum*, London (1957 8–1.1) CENTRE LEFT The framework only of an ornamental detail from a Koran produced in Iraq or Iran 1073–4. *Mashad Shrine Library* (4316 ff. 2v–3r); RIGHT the framework only of an ornamental detail from a Koran produced in Iraq or Iran in 1092. *Collection of Aga Mahdi Kashani*, Teheran. BOTTOM Roundels with a diameter of only 1.6 cm under the rim of a brass ewer made in Mosul, Iraq in 1232 are made up of two different—but very similar-looking—interlaced designs. Both are illustrated here: LEFT one half of each as they appear, RIGHT showing their construction. *British Museum*, London (1866 12–29.61).

57 TOP The framework only of an ornamental detail from a Koran produced in Valencia, Spain in 1182–3. *University Library*, Istanbul (A6754 f. 131v). BOTTOM Design inside a bronze bowl. Diameter 7 cm. Khurasan, Iran, early 13th century, *Victoria and Albert Museum*, London (M. 388–1911).

58 TOP and CENTRE RIGHT Designs from tooled and gilt leather bookbindings. Shown approximately 2:1. Egypt, 14th century. *British Library*, London (Or. 848). CENTRE LEFT Design from tooled leather bookbinding. Diameter 6 cm. Egypt, 15th century. *Victoria and Albert Museum*, London (366/2–1888). BOTTOM Punched engraved and inlaid design from a bronze bucket. 6 × 6 cm. East? Persia/Afghanistan, 12th century. *British Museum*, London (1969 6–19.1).

59 TOP Design on a bronze dish, engraved and inlaid in silver. Diameter of design 10.7 cm. Khurasan, Iran, late 12th century. *Victoria and Albert Museum*, London (548–1876). BOTTOM Designs from tooled and gilt leather bookbindings. LEFT Diameter 8.3 cm. North Africa, 15th century. RIGHT Diameter 9.7 cm. Egypt/Syria, 14th–15th centuries. *The Oriental Institute*, The University of Chicago (A 12154 and 12156).

60–61 Earthenware dishes moulded in low relief, with yellow lead glaze and lustre with touches of green. Iraq, 9th century. **60** Diameter 21.7 cm. *Staatliche Museen Preussischer Kulturbesitz, Museum für Islamische Kunst*, Berlin–Dahlem (Bab. 2969). **61** *Freer Gallery of Art*, Washington DC (57.23).

62 TOP Openwork panel from the side of a brass incense burner. length of panel aproximately 10 cm. *British Museum*, London (1956 7–26.6). BOTTOM Detail of openwork from incense burner. Width of border 9 cm. Khurasan, Iran, 10th century. *Victoria and Albert Museum*, London (unnumbered).

63 TOP Details of the design on earthenware dishes decorated in coloured slips under a clear lead glaze.

LEFT Diameter of motif approximately 23 cm. Iran, 10th century. *Freer Gallery of Art*, Washington DC (57.24); RIGHT East Iran or Transoxiana. *Metropolitan Museum of Art*, New York (40.170.15). BOTTOM Design on an earthenware dish painted in black and red slips on a cream ground under a clear lead glaze. Diameter 28.5 cm. East Iran or Transoxiana, 10th–11th centuries. *The Keir Collection*, London (61).

64 Extended drawing of the engraved and inlaid design on a brass candle-stick. Northern Mesopotamia?, 13th century. *British Museum*, London (1955 2–14.2).

65 Extended drawing of the engraved and inlaid design on a brass candle-stick. Siirt, southeast Turkey, early 14th century. *Nuhad Es-Said Collection*.

66–67 Details from a Koran produced in Iran in 1313. *National Library*, Cairo (Koran 72).

68 Details of designs on pottery painted in lustre on white tin glaze. Iraq, 9th–10th centuries. LEFT *Freer Gallery of Art*, Washington DC (53–90). RIGHT TOP Diameter of detail approximately 22 cm. *David Collection*, Copenhagen (14/1962); BOTTOM Diameter 28.7 cm. *British Museum*, London (1968 10–15.1).

69 TOP LEFT Design on bowl painted in lustre on a white glaze. Iraq, 10th century. *David Collection*, Copenhagen (26/1962); RIGHT the central motif of a bowl painted in lustre on a white glaze. Iran, 9th–10th centuries. *Iran Bastan Museum*, Teheran (3050). BOTTOM Design painted on a bowl in olive green on a white slip. Diameter 24 cm. Nishapur, Iran, 10th century. *British Museum*, London (1970 7–17.1).

70–71 *Chester Beatty Library*, Dublin (1431).

72 TOP LEFT Detail of the design on a bowl painted in black slip on a white ground under a clear glaze. East Iran or Transoxiana, 10th century. *Victoria and Albert Museum*, London (C. 92–1969); RIGHT detail of the design on a bowl painted in lustre. Egypt or Syria, mid-12th century. *Metropolitan Museum of Art*, New York (66.37). CENTRE Detail of the design on a potsherd painted in black slip on a white ground. Nishapur, Iran, 10th century. *Metropolitan Museum of Art*, New York (40.170.564). BOTTOM LEFT Detail of the design on a bowl painted in lustre. Iran, late 12th century. *National Museum*, Damascus (A 14294); RIGHT detail of the design on a bowl carved in low relief under a blue glaze. Iran, mid-12th century. *Victoria and Albert Museum*, London (C. 68–1931).

73 The bowls on which these designs occur were covered with a thick black slip which was cut away to expose the white frit ware underneath. They were then glazed with a clear or turquoise-coloured transparent glaze. TOP LEFT Diameter 13.9 cm. *Keir Collection*, London (130); RIGHT Diameter 17 cm. *Victoria and Albert Museum*, London (C. 20–1956). BOTTOM Diameter of the design 18.5 cm. *Ashmolean Museum*, Oxford (1956.130). Iran, second half 12th century.

74 Details of designs painted in black on white frit ware under a clear alkaline glaze on bowls from the early 13th century in Kashan, Iran. TOP *Victoria and Albert Museum*, London; BOTTOM *Museum of Fine Arts*, Boston (65.230).

75 TOP Design inside a bowl, the plant ornament painted in black, the cross in blue (indicated by a screen) under a clear alkaline glaze. Diameter 20.5 cm. BELOW A section of a scroll painted in black under a turquoise clear glaze from the outside of a bowl. Kashan, Iran, c. 1200. *Ashmolean Museum*, Oxford (1978.2255 and 1956.29).

76 *British Library*, London (Add. 22406/7).

77 TOP Shallow frit ware dish, covered with opaque turquoise glaze and painted overglaze in white, black and red. Diameter 20.5 cm. Iran, mid-13th century. *Freer Gallery of Art*, Washington DC (op. 112). BOTTOM The two roundels decorate a small silver bowl: on the outside the countersunk base is decorated with an engraved and punched design LEFT which also appears in repoussé on a disc which covers the inside of the base RIGHT. *Private collection*.

78–79 See **76**.

80 *British Library*, London (Or. 4945 frontispiece).

81 See **66–67**.

82 TOP Egypt/Syria/South Arabia (Yemen), 14th–15th centuries. BOTTOM Actual size of the repeat 18 cm square. Egypt, 1401. *Victoria and Albert Museum*, London (1951–1981 and 387–1898).

83 TOP height of repeat approximately 11 cm. South Arabia/(Yemen). 15th century. *Oriental Institute*, The University of Chicago (A 12134). BOTTOM Egypt/Syria, 14th century. *Victoria and Albert Museum*, London (88–1880).

84 Details from a writing-box inlaid with silver and gold (indicated here by a screen). Diameter of roundel 6.4 cm. Egypt, c. 1300–1350. *British Museum*, London (81 8–2.20).

85 TOP Design from a brass basin inlaid with silver, gold (indicated here by a screen) and a black bituminous material. Inlaid material has been reconstructed in the drawing. Diameter 12.5 cm. Egypt or Syria, c. 1330–1340. *British Museum*, London (51 1–4.1). BOTTOM Borders from the frontispieces of Korans. Cairo, 14th century. *National Library*, Cairo (Koran 54 and 7).

86 Border tiles painted in dark and light blue, green and strong red. *Saz* means reed or rush, but the leaves which bear this name in Islamic decoration clearly bear no relationship to a living plant. Length of tiles from the top: 24 cm, 26 cm, 32 cm. Iznik, Turkey, second half of the 16th century. *Çinili Köşk Museum*, Istanbul.

87 Panel of polychrome tiles from the bath of the Great Mosque at Eyüp, Istanbul. Each tile is 26.5 cm square. Iznik, Turkey, 1560–1580. *Victoria and Albert Museum*, London (401–1900).

88 Dish painted in blue, turquoise and grey-green on

white. Diameter 37 cm. Iznik, Turkey, c. 1540. *Victoria and Albert Museum*, London (c. 1995–1910). Screens are used here to indicate different colours. This does not mean that a particular screen always represents the same colour; the screens merely serve to give an impression of the way light and dark shades are distributed in the designs. Colours tend to a naturalistic choice of, for example, red for roses and green for leaves, but there are many exceptions to this rule. Shades of blue are by far the dominant colour.

89 Dish. Diameter 27.6 cm. Iznik, Turkey, mid-16th century. *Private collection*. On the use of screens see **88**.

90 Dish painted in blue, black, green and red. Diameter 26.3 cm. Iznik, Turkey, second half of the 16th century. *Private collection*. On the use of screens see **88**.

91 Dish. Diameter 33.7 cm. Iznik, Turkey, 1570–1600. *British Museum*, London (F.B. 1S.4.). On the use of screens see **88**.

92 Dish. Diameter 31.4 cm. Iznik, Turkey, 1570–1600. *British Museum*, London (78 12–30.484). On the use of screens see **88**.

93 Dish. Diameter 28 cm. Iznik, Turkey, c. 1550. *British Museum*, London. (78 12–30.527). On the use of screens see **88**.

94 Tinned copper dish cover with engraved design. Western Iran, c. 1590–1600. *Victoria and Albert Museum*, London (M. 177–1976).

95 Polychrome border tiles. Iznik, Turkey, second half of the 16th century. TOP and CENTRE, 25 × 14 cm and 31 × 22 cm. *Çinili Köşk Museum*, Istanbul. BOTTOM 24.7 cm square. *British Museum*, London (96 6–3.146).

96 Polychrome tiles. TOP 25 cm square. BOTTOM 28 × 7 cm. Iznik, Turkey, second half of the 16th century. *Private collections*.

97 TOP Polychrome tile from the Rüstem Paşa Mosque built in 1561, Istanbul. BOTTOM Border tile painted in black, green, blue and red. 15 × 14.5 cm. Iznik, Turkey, c. 1560–80. Left hand tile *British Museum*, London (95 6–3.148) right hand tile reconstructed to complete the repeat design.

98–99 Engraved and punched designs from Ottoman brass candle-sticks of the late 15th or early 16th centuries. **98** and last border on **99** *Victoria and Albert Museum*, London (411f–1880), remaining three borders **99** *Freer Gallery of Art*, Washington DC (80.19).

100 TOP Hexagonal tile painted in manganese purple, shown here as black, with small circles in pale blue or green, indicated here by a screen. The design is outlined in black. Maximum measurement of tile 27 cm. Damascus, second half of the 16th century. *Private collection*. BOTTOM Border tile. Design outlined in black, background dark blue, small dots pale green. Length 27.2 cm. Damascus, Syria 17th century. *British Museum*, London (84 10–17.1).

Further reading

Bourgoin, J. *Arabic geometrical pattern and design*, Dover Pictorial Archive Series, New York 1973. This is a reprint of the plates from *Les Éléments de l'art Arabe . . .* originally published in Paris 1879.

Caiger-Smith, A. *Tin-Glaze Pottery, in Europe and the Islamic World*, London 1973.

Caiger-Smith, A. *Lustre Pottery, Technique, Tradition and Innovation in Islam and the Western World*, London 1985.

Critchlow, K. *Islamic Patterns. An Analytical and Cosmological Approach*, London 1976.

Dilke, O. A. W. *Mathematics and Measurements*, Reading the Past, London 1987.

Elgood R. ed. *Islamic Arms and Armour*, London 1979.

El-Said, I. and Parman, A. *Geometric Concepts in Islamic Art*, London 1976.

Erdmann, K. *Seven hundred years of Oriental Carpets*, London 1970.

Gombrich, E. H. *The Sense of Order. A study in the psychology of decorative art*, London 1984.

Goodwin, G. *A History of Ottoman Architecture*, London 1987.

Grube, E. J. *The World of Islam*, Landmarks in the World's Art, London 1966.

Lane, A. *Early Islamic Pottery*, London 1947.

Lewis, B. ed. *The World of Islam*, London 1976.

Lings, M. *The Quranic Art of Calligraphy and Illumination*, London 1976.

Rice, D. Talbot *Islamic Art*, London 1984.

Robinson, F. *Atlas of the Islamic World since 1500*, Oxford 1982.

Rogers, J. M. *Islamic Art and Design 1500–1700*, London 1983.

Safadi, Y. H. *Islamic Calligraphy*, London 1978.

Seherr-Thoss, S. P. *Design and Colour in Islamic Architecture*, Washington 1968.

Watson, O. *Persian Lustre Ware*, London 1985.

The
Designs

1 Birds painted on a 10th-century pottery dish with the word *blessing* inscribed on their bodies.

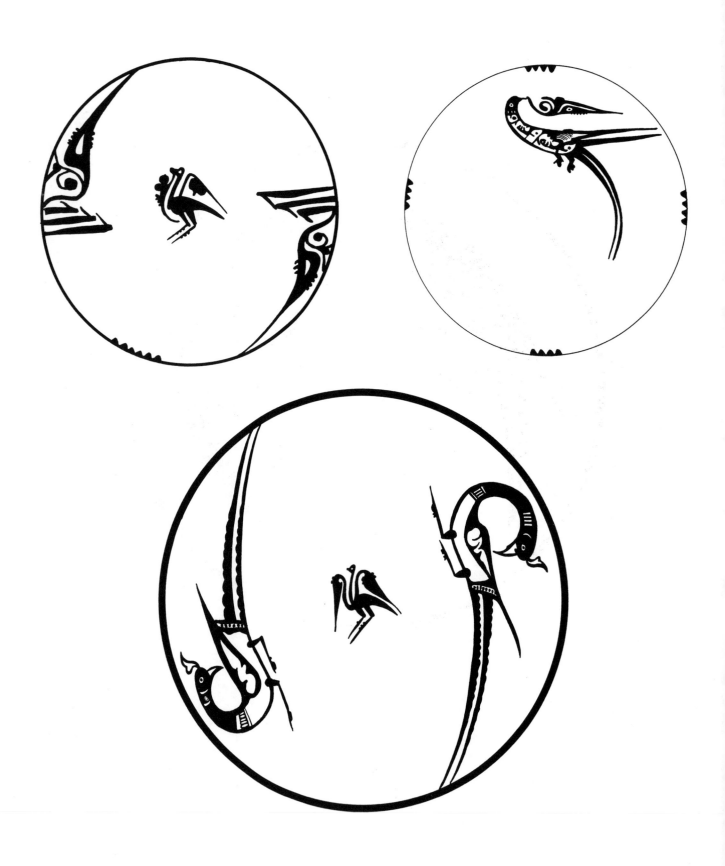

2 Bird motifs painted on pottery go back to pre-Islamic Sasanian art and may symbolise good fortune. The repeated design at the rim TOP LEFT, however, is the word *Allah*, reduced to three strokes and a flourish. Iran, 10th century.

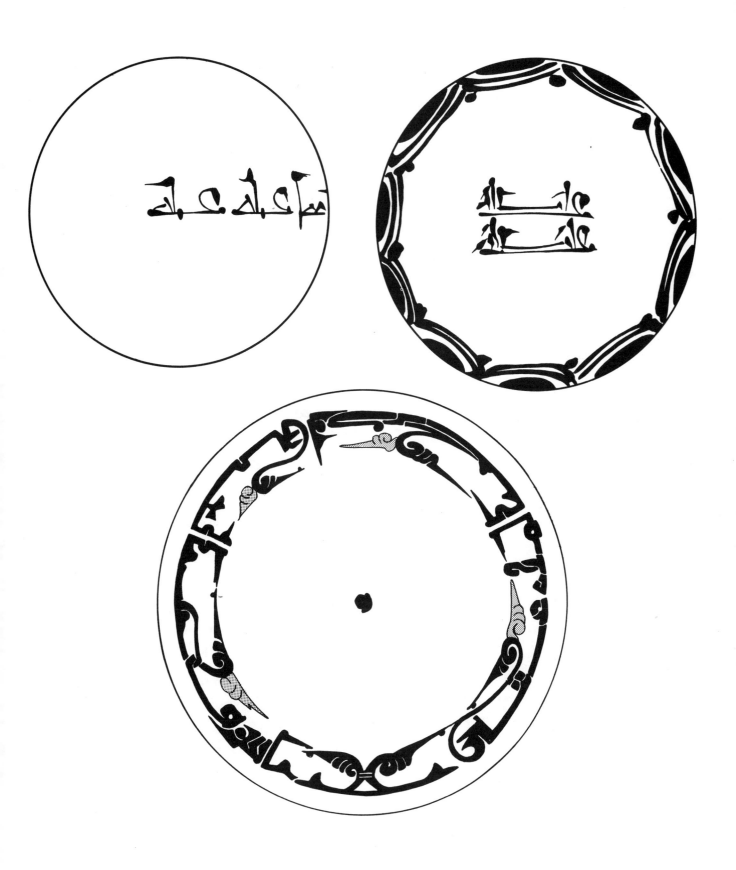

3 The decorative use of calligraphy became the most distinctive element in Islamic art. On domestic pottery the inscriptions are usually blessings or sometimes names. TOP Iraq, BOTTOM Iran, 9th–10th centuries.

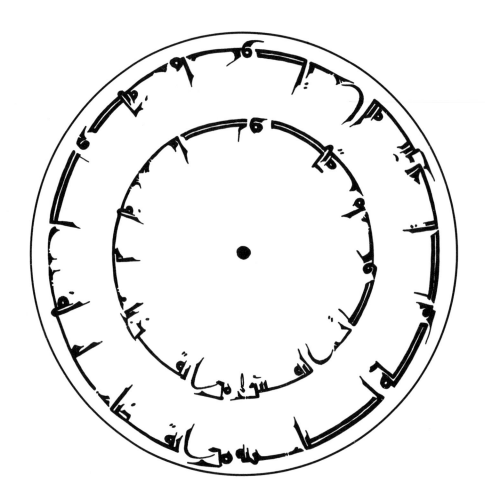

4 Decorative forms of Kufic script: TOP on pottery, BOTTOM LEFT engraved and inlaid on metal and RIGHT carved in stone. The inscription TOP reads: *He who professes the faith will excel; and to whatever you accustom yourself you will grow accustomed to. Blessing to the owner.*

5 Decorative forms of Kufic script; TOP on pottery, BOTTOM LEFT carved in wood and RIGHT on a glazed tile. The inscription reads: *Allah, there is no God but He*, this is repeated on each side of the tile with the high risers forming an interlocking pattern in the centre. The word *He* is superimposed in a contrasting colour (indicated by a screen).

6 Thuluth was the cursive script most frequently used for decorative purposes—typically set against a background of scroll work. TOP on a tile, CENTRE carved on an ivory panel. BOTTOM the inscription carved in marble: *There is no god but God and Muhammad is the Prophet of God*. Egypt, 13th–15th centuries.

7 Openwork steel door panel with a Thuluth inscription. Isfahan?, Iran, 1693–4.

8 Textile designs may have influenced the decoration on the 10th-century dish from Iraq BOTTOM, which also bears the inscription *blessings to the owner*. Such wares were exported to eastern Iran where more stylised designs were produced TOP.

9 Animal symbolism was common everywhere in the ancient world. However, the significance of these attractive and popular motifs on domestic pottery from Iran is not known. 10th–13th centuries.

10 Shoals of fish decorate the inside of many metal or pottery bowls, often in a rotating design. The roundel TOP RIGHT includes the zodiac sign Pisces.

11 Animals of the hunt are represented in a conventionalised naturalistic style in the classical tradition. The hare is painted on pottery TOP RIGHT from 11th-century Egypt, CENTRE 12th-century Syria and TOP LEFT 12th-century Iran. The hare BOTTOM is engraved on the rim of a metal dish from Iran, late 12th or early 13th century.

12 While animal and human figures rarely occur in religious contexts, many domestic objects are decorated with such motifs. Designs painted on lustre pottery from 10th-century Iraq, however, include a religious evocation TOP: *trust* (in God) *and* (leaving the reader to complete a text from the Koran) . . . *he will be sufficient for you.*

13 The design BOTTOM, painted in lustre on a dish from 12th-century Syria, shows a prince seated on a stool or throne. His royal status is indicated by the cup in his hand. It is possible that such scenes referred to epic stories.

14 The designs on this large bowl and that OPPOSITE are reserved in the white glaze against a painted background of brownish-gold lustre. Iran, late 12th or early 13th centuries.

15 These large and complex designs are fitted into small and confined spaces with great skill.

16 The scenes on this page and that OPPOSITE decorate a brass ewer dated by inscription to 1232 at Mosul, Iraq. The beaten brass of the ewer is engraved and inlaid with silver and copper (indicated here by a screen). 2:1.

17 The motifs depict life at court, fighting and hunting. Halos do not indicate holiness in Islamic art. 2:1.

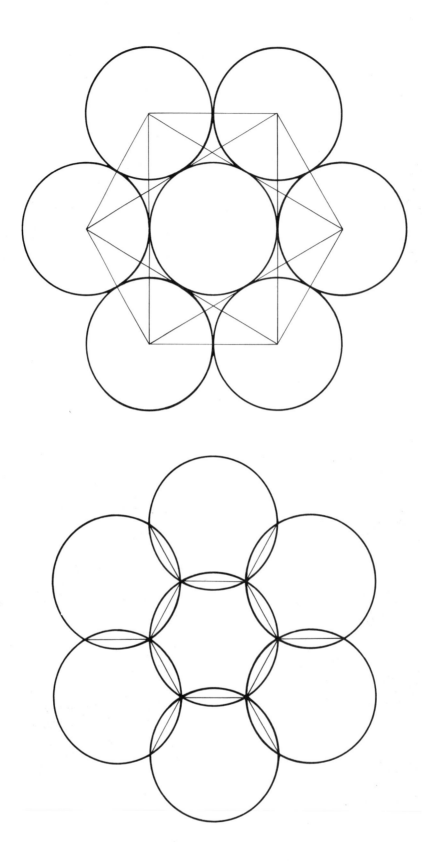

18 A circle surrounded by six circles of the same size produces a hexagon-based pattern. This seven-circles pattern is commonly used in Islamic art, both as a design in its own right and as a grid for pattern-making. (After Critchlow 1976).

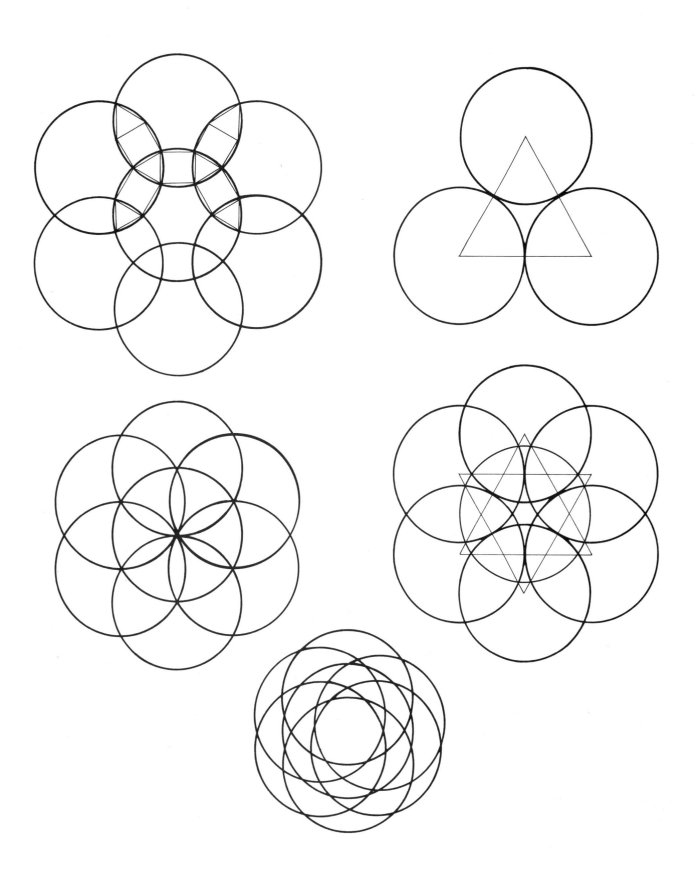

19 As the peripheral circles encroach on the inner circle, different configurations are produced with a variety of geometric and decorative characteristics. (After Critchlow 1976).

20 Examples of designs based on the seven-circles pattern from Khurasan in eastern Iran. TOP on pottery, BOTTOM from a plaster panel in low relief. 10th century.

21 TOP The design engraved on a brass plate is analysed BELOW to show the underlying seven-circles pattern. Actual size. Iran, 10th–11th centuries.

22 Variations on the seven-circles pattern from different parts of the Islamic world. LEFT designs on pottery, RIGHT a design in tooled leather from a bookbinding.

23 More complicated designs showing BELOW the seven-circles grid on which they may have been drawn. LEFT from Khurasan, eastern Iran, RIGHT from Egypt. 14th century.

24 This design, engraved on a large metal dish from Iran, is based on a pattern of eight circles which surrounds a central circle of the same size. Late 12th or early 13th centuries.

25 Designs on earthenware bowls are incised through a white slip under a transparent glaze. The technique and the design appear to be derived from engraved metalwork. Iran, 10th–12th centuries.

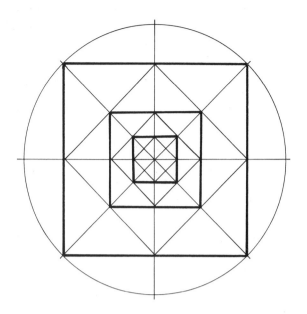

When lengths of the sides of concentric squares inscribed in a circle are related by the proportion of 1:√2 the areas are progressively halved.

When the length of the sides are halved the areas are quartered.

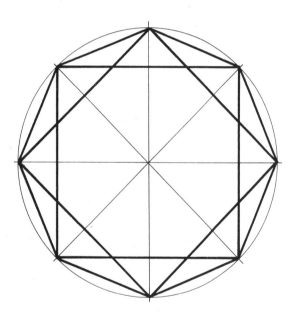

The octagon and the eight-pointed star.

When eight-pointed stars are set consecutively so that the lengths of consecutive parallel sides are related by the proportion of 1:√2, lengths of alternative sides are halved.

26 Some of the constructions and properties of squares, octagons and eight-pointed stars used in geometric designs. (After El-Said and Parman 1976).

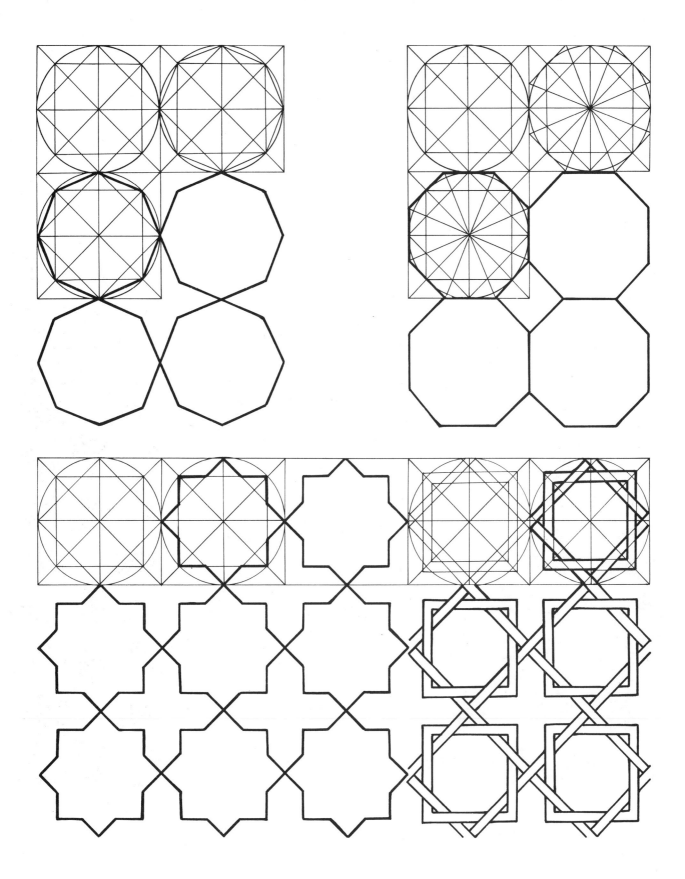

27 Geometric designs typically cover entire areas with a framework creating shapes often filled with other motifs such as leaf scrolls. One method of producing such frameworks uses repeat units based on a geometric grid. These examples of simple repeat patterns are drawn on octagon-based grids. (After El-Said and Parman 1976).

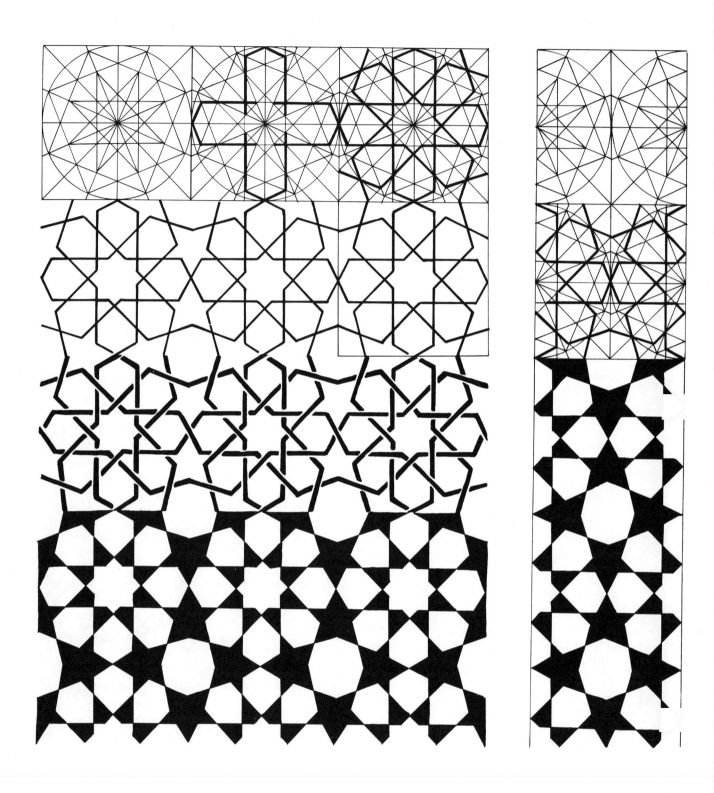

28 A variety of repeat patterns may be produced on the basis of the same grid. The top
row of the design LEFT shows the development of the repeat unit from the grid. The
design RIGHT shows a modification of this repeat unit in which the two halves are set
back to back, producing a border design. (After El-Said and Parman 1976).

29 The repeat unit is here based on the same basic grid as OPPOSITE but is set within a rectangle. This method allows almost unlimited scope for variation and the resulting repeat patterns were developed in Islamic art in many different ways to create a rich variety of designs. (After El-Said and Parman 1976).

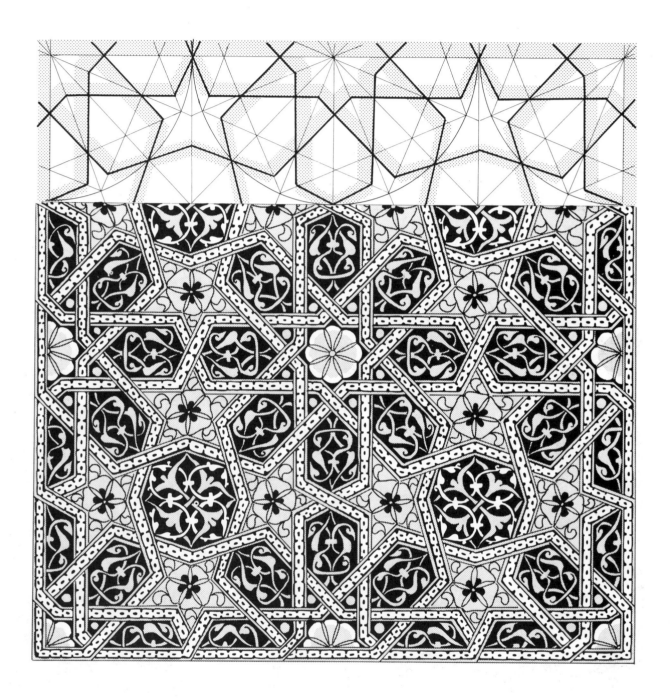

30 Detail from a Koran illumination based on the grid shown at 28. The slimmer shape of the star's rays and the smaller central octagon are produced by positioning the interlacing ribbon over the grid as shown TOP, i.e. with the grid line either in the centre or to one side of the ribbon, a device which allows for further variations in designs of this kind. Egypt, 15th century.

31 Small interlaced motifs based on squares, octagons and four-fold divisions.

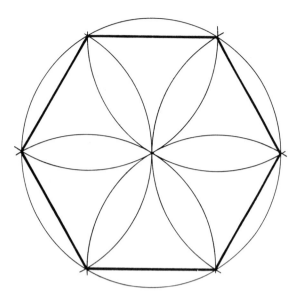

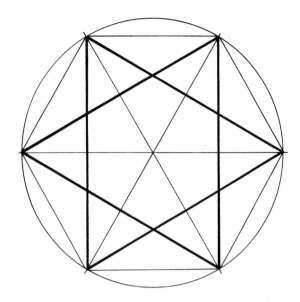

The circumference of a circle can be divided into six equal parts by its radius. When the six points set off on the circumference are joined by straight lines a hexagon is produced.

When alternative points are joined by straight lines two triangles are produced which together make up a six-pointed star.

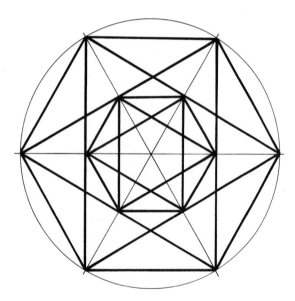

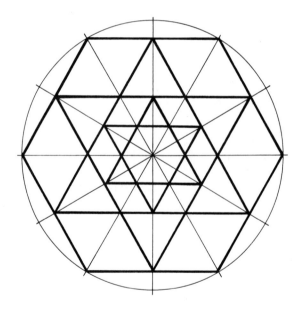

The ratio between the diameters of hexagons based on concentric six-pointed stars drawn from the hexagon's corners is 1:2.

When the concentric stars are drawn from the hexagon's midpoints, the ratio between the heights of the hexagons is also 1:2. The ratio between the diameter and the height of a hexagon is √3:2.

32 Some of the constructions and properties of the hexagon and the six-pointed star used in geometric designs. This is the most important geometrical figure in Islamic art. (After El-Said and Parman 1976).

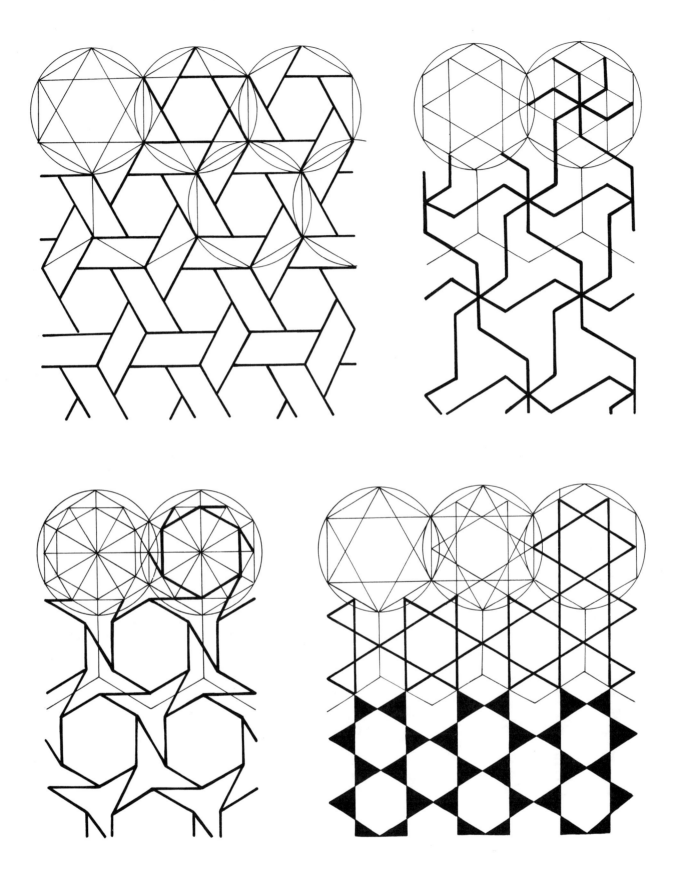

33 The hexagon itself serves as a versatile repeat unit. It is the most common basis for repeat patterns and many designs of apparently very different character are drawn on hexagon-based grids. (After El-Said and Parman 1976).

34 The repeat unit of this design is constructed in two stages: in the top line the hexagonal double frame is based on two hexagons, in the second line the star is drawn on a grid of three squares (After El-Said and Parman 1976).

35 Detail from a Koran frontispiece with a design laid out on a grid similar, though not identical, to that shown OPPOSITE. Egypt, 1356.

36 In the 15th-century Mosque at Edirne in Turkey, hexagonal tiles decorated in blue and white are set in a pattern with plain turquoise triangular tiles.

37 A hexagonal tile can serve as a repeat unit by itself. Such densely decorated tiles, which are capable of repeating their designs in all directions as demonstrated here, may also be set with triangular spacers as shown OPPOSITE.

38 These patterns are representative of a large group of common hexagonal-based Islamic designs. The design RIGHT demonstrates that this could also be drawn on a grid of triangles like the border BOTTOM. (After El-Said and Parman 1976).

39 The engraved and inlaid border from a brass writing box BOTTOM shows this type of design used as a space-filler. The roundels, also taken from metal objects, demonstrate how the design can be made to 'rotate'. A grid on which the large roundel can be drawn is shown CENTRE.

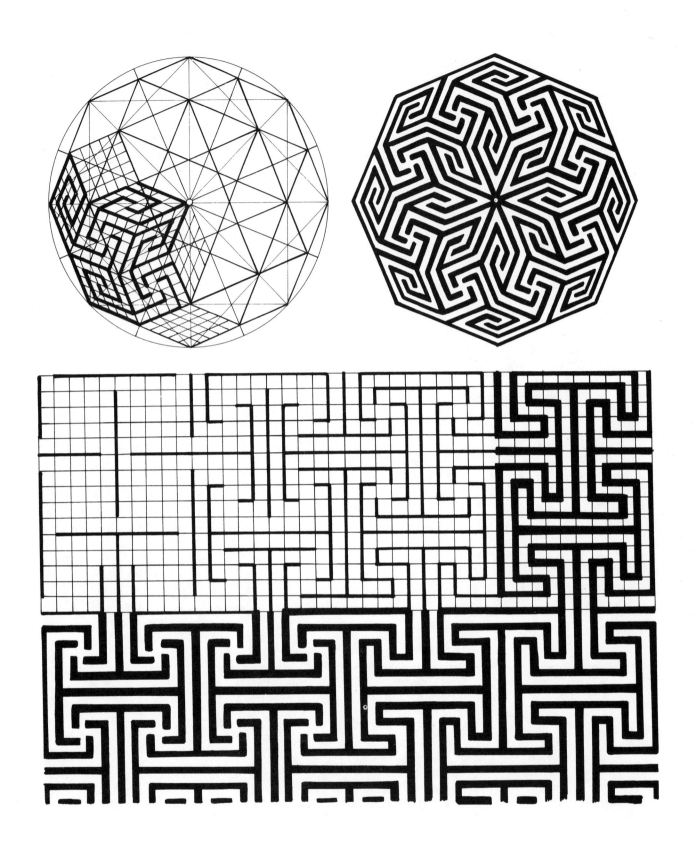

40 Key patterns have ancient origins and are not exclusive to Islamic art. They can be drawn on several types of geometric grids, examples of which are shown here.

41 Key patterns, Y-patterns and rotating patterns are mostly used as space-fillers. These examples are all from engraved and inlaid designs on metalwork.

42 Rotating designs are common in Islamic art from all periods and regions and in many media. The designs shown here range from Egypt to Transoxiana and from the 10th to the 13th centuries. They are painted on pottery, cast in bronze and engraved and inlaid in metal.

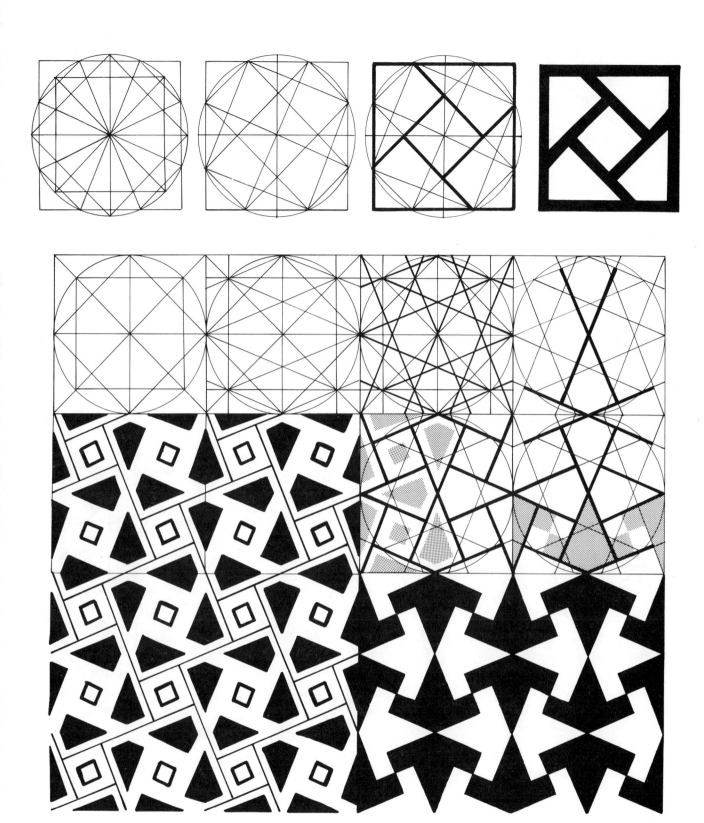

43 TOP a rotating motif constructed as a single unit on an octagon-based grid. BELOW: when this motif is constructed as a repeat pattern its gridlines (shown without the lines of construction in the last three squares) allow for different variations of the design to be drawn, as shown by two examples. (After El-Said and Parman 1976).

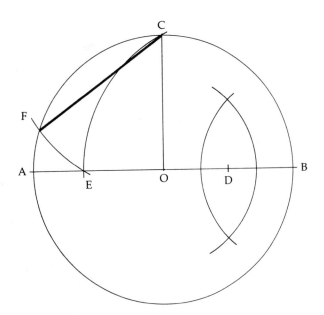

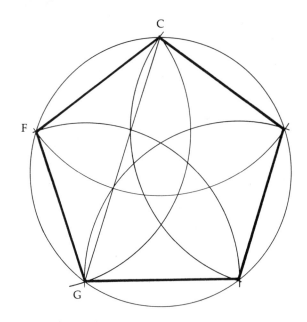

To construct a pentagon inscribed in a circle: bisect OB at D; with centre D and radius DC cut OA at E; with centre C and radius CE cut the circumference at F; FC equals one side of the pentagon. Complete the pentagon by dividing the circumference into five equal parts, each the length of FC. The ratio of the diagonal GC to the side FC in a regular pentagon is 1:1.618 or Ø (the Golden Mean).

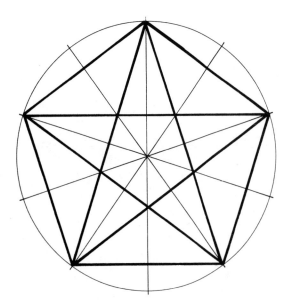

The pentagon and the five-pointed star.

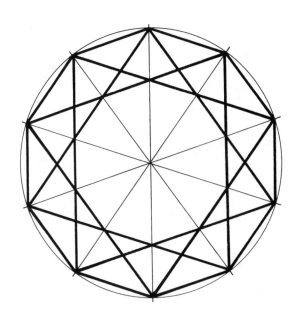

The decagon and the ten-pointed star.

44 Some constructions and properties of the pentagon, decagon and the five- and ten-pointed star used in geometric design. The ratios within the pentagon gave rise to great interest in the ancient and Islamic worlds as they conform to the proportion known as the Golden Mean (After El-Said and Parman 1976).

45 LEFT A repeat unit based on the ten-pointed star has a grid composed of parallel lines running in five directions. Enclosed in a square, this unit will not repeat sideways (see also 46–7). RIGHT Common decorative motifs based on extending the lines of a ten-pointed star. (After El-Said and Parman 1976 and Critchlow 1976).

46 A grid based on the ten-pointed star can be made to repeat in all directions by inscribing it in a shape such as a rectangle. (After El-Said and Parman 1976).

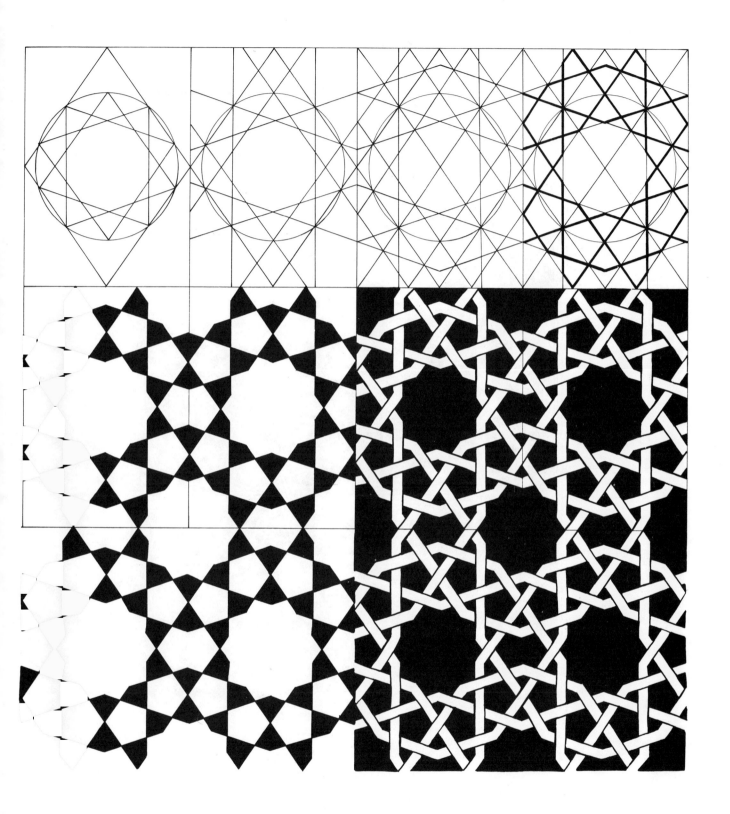

47 When the same ten-pointed star grid is inscribed in a rhomboid within a rectangle, a different pattern may be drawn on the resulting grid. A common treatment of the final design is interlacing which gives it a three-dimensional character. Varying the widths of the interlacing ribbons produces further variations in these designs. (After El-Said and Parman 1976).

48 Detail of a Koran frontispiece based on a decagon grid. Egypt, 14th century.

49 Two designs based on similar ten-pointed star grids. TOP is the framework of a design on a tooled leather bookbinding from 15th-century Turkey; possible lines of construction are shown LEFT. BELOW is the detail from a frontispiece of a 14th-century Koran written in Egypt.

50 Copies of the Koran are often prefaced by richly-decorated frontispieces. Some decoration also occurs on the pages of text. These designs feature interlaced borders and panels.

51 The interlacing ribbons are usually painted in gold with touches of blue and red (indicated by a screen). These examples, and the two borders BOTTOM OPPOSITE, are taken from a 10th-century Koran probably written in Egypt.

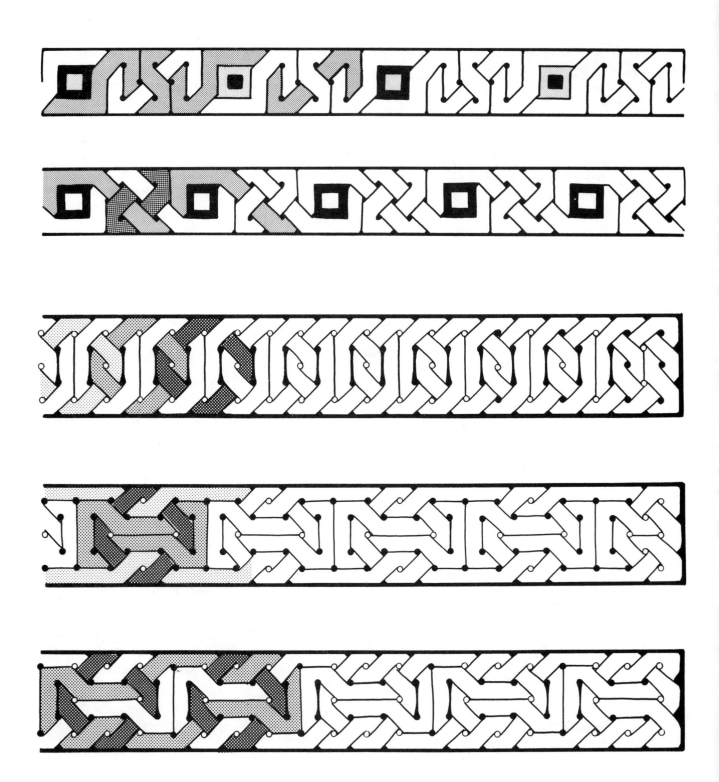

52 Ribbon interlace from a Koran produced in Cairo in 1304. The three borders BOTTOM OPPOSITE are taken from the same work. The different methods used – as analysed left – demonstrate the various ways in which similar effects were achieved. 2:1.

53 The ribbons are painted in gold. The small circles where the ribbons cross are picked out in blue and red. The circles may have helped in the construction of the interlace, or they may mimic the stamped circles on leather bookbindings with similar designs. 2:1.

54 TOP Three, four and six-strand interlace borders turning corners. The border BOTTOM
is made up of a sequence of two closed loops and two ribbons interlacing as shown.
From Korans of the 13th and 14th centuries.

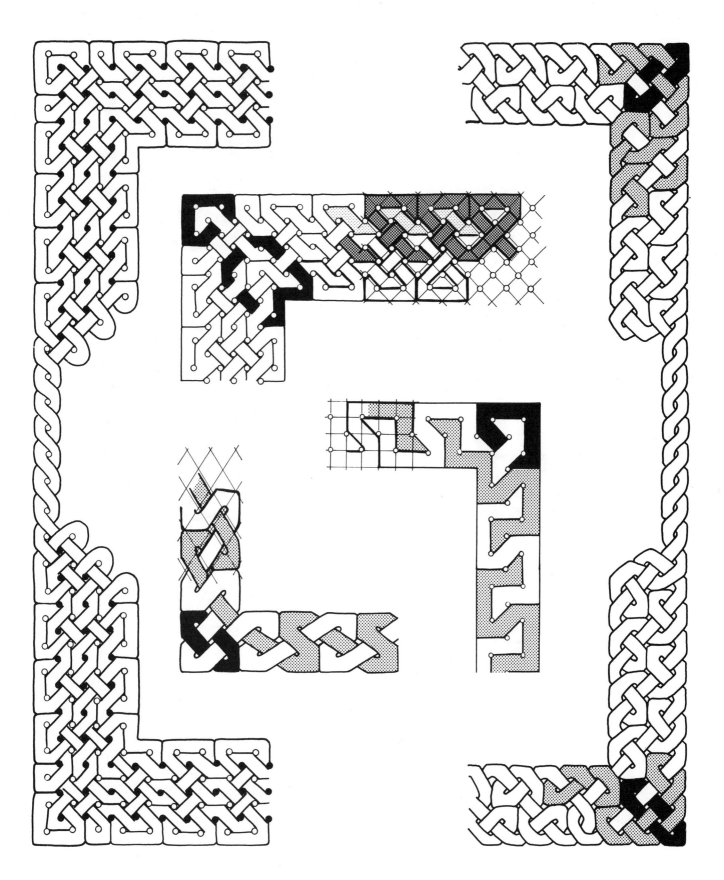

55 The corners of interlaced borders are not always turned in a regular manner or in the same way in all the corners of the same border RIGHT. The technique of turning corners by inserting a closed loop is further demonstrated LEFT (analysed TOP CENTRE) and BELOW CENTRE. From Korans of the 14th–15th centuries.

56 Interlaced circular designs are extremely common motifs in Islamic art. These examples are based on the six-pointed star and are taken from manuscripts and metal-work.

57 These intricate designs, TOP from a manuscript and BOTTOM engraved in a bronze bowl, are shown, on analysis, to have a common feature: the underlying octagonal or hexagonal grids are encircled by interlacing elements which suggest a flower effect. Some of the simpler designs OPPOSITE show the same characteristic.

58 TOP, CENTRE and BOTTOM OPPOSITE, Stamped designs on tooled leather bookbindings. Two stamps only, a bar and an arc, are used to produce the interlaced designs. BOTTOM Punched and engraved designs on metalwork often use similar motifs to those on leather and achieve similar effects.

59 Analysis of the design on a late 12th-century bronze dish from Khurasan, Iran, TOP, reveals the petal-like ribbons which are interlaced with the six-pointed star.

60 The distinction between abstract patterns and plant motifs become less clear when plant elements grow out of interlace. On this dish and OPPOSITE, palmette motifs of the Sasanian tradition develop from a late Classical type of interlace.

61 On this early type of moulded pottery from 9th-century Iraq, the dishes are painted in lustre over a lead glaze, evidently to simulate the appearance of the metal dishes from which they so clearly derive their designs.

62 Details of interlace and palmette ornament in openwork on 10th-century incense burners. The palmettes link the interlacing ribbons in a variety of ways.

63 Details of combined interlace and palmette motifs on pottery. The interlacing ribbons take on the character of intertwined plant stems.

64 Extended drawing of the design engraved and inlaid on the drum-shaped base of a brass candle-stick. The interlacing ribbons surround rosettes: a universal motif based on a stereotyped flower.

65 Extended drawing of the design engraved and inlaid on the drum-shaped base of a brass candle-stick. The rosettes are surrounded by an intricate interlace based on an elongated hexagon which is analysed below.

66 Details from a Koran written and illuminated in Iran in 1313. The disciplined structure of the interlace combines with leaves, based on the palmette motif, to produce a versatile ornament which fills the different shapes created by the rigid geometric framework.

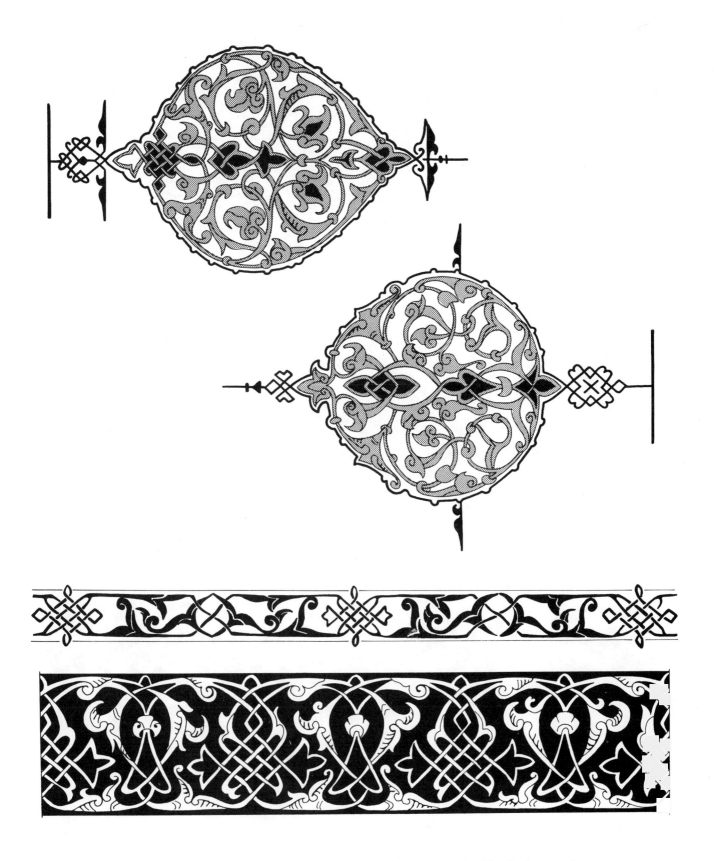

67 The beginning of a chapter in illuminated Korans was marked by designs such as those TOP which extended into the margin. These examples, from the same book as the designs OPPOSITE, are painted in gold (indicated by a screen) with touches of blue (shown here black).

68 It appears that nobody in the ancient world drew plant ornament from nature: leaves and flowers were highly stylised and based on traditional forms.

69 Designs painted on 9th- and 10th-century pottery from Iraq are made up of split and interlocking palmettes.

70 and OPPOSITE Designs from a Koran written and illuminated by Ibn al-Bawwab in Baghdad *c.* 1000 illustrate the most important motifs in Islamic plant ornament: the oriental and Egyptian lotus motifs, the rosette, the split palmette scroll and the palmette flower.

71 These designs, which mark chapter headings in the margins of the same Koran as OPPOSITE, show winged designs typical of the Sasanian tradition.

72 Palmette leaf scrolls painted or inscribed on pottery. 9th–12th centuries.

73 Palmette flowers and leaf designs on pottery. Iran 12th century.

74 For a short period in the early 13th century the 'water weed' design became a popular motif in Kashan, Iran. The discovery of a clear alkaline glaze, which allowed painting directly on the white frit ware without the colours spreading during firing, made it possible to produce such elegant designs.

75 Although this motif sometimes occurs together with fishes (10 CENTRE) it is unlikely that it represents any particular aquatic plant. The designs conform to the traditional scroll form or are arranged with stylised symmetry.

76 These designs, taken from a Koran produced in Cairo in 1304, illustrate the style of leaf scroll, made up mainly of split palmette leaves, which became known as *arabesque*. The text which overlays the scroll BOTTOM is what is often described as Eastern Kufic script.

77 The designs on a 13th-century pottery dish from Iran TOP and on a silver bowl from the late 15th or early 16th centuries BOTTOM illustrate what is generally known as the *arabesque style.*

78 Detail of a border from a Koran written and illuminated in Cairo in 1304. On the left a portion of the border has been analysed to show the construction of the intricate design.

79 The scroll work in this design from the same Koran as in 76 and OPPOSITE is painted in gold with blue (shown here as black) and red (indicated by a screen). The text in white Thuluth script reads: [the] *seven*.

80 Detail from the frontispiece of a Koran produced in Mosul in 1310. The leaf scrolls in the hexagons are painted in gold against a blue background (shown here as black) or a red background (indicated by a screen). The borders are in gold and pale green.

81 Detail from the frontispiece of a Koran produced in Iran in 1313. In the centre is a white ribbon interlace and leaf scroll on a blue ground; the designs in the hexagons are painted in black and in the eight-sided shapes in gold against a natural background.

82 Designs block-printed on thin leather which lined the boards of bookbindings. Arrows indicate the joins between repeat units where they can be observed. 14th–15th centuries.

83 The leather was printed with a tanning agent which produced a darker background colour.

84 The formalised oriental lotus is one of the few truly floral motifs in Islamic decorative art before the Ottoman period. These designs are taken from a writing box inlaid with silver and gold from 14th-century Egypt.

85 In these designs, which show a strong Chinese influence, formalised and composite flowers are set in the traditional scroll pattern. TOP engraved in metal; BOTTOM painted in borders from a Koran. Egypt, 14th century.

86 The traditional floral scroll featuring composite flowers and *saz* leaves continued to be one of the common motifs in the ceramic production at Iznik during the Ottoman Empire. These border tiles were painted in dark and light blue, green and strong red. Second half of the 16th century.

87 The panel of tiles painted in blue, green and red is made up of just two tile patterns, each the mirror image of the other (A and B). Together they create a very rich design typical of the 'enchanted forest' effect of the *saz* style. Iznik, Turkey, 1560–1580.

88 The colourful 16th-century pottery of Ottoman Turkey introduced lavish plant ornament. The basic tree or spray, rooted on the edge of the dish, led to a wide range of
different uses of the limited space.

89 On this dish composite flowers made up of petals, buds and leaves are arranged in a rotating pattern interspersed with *saz* leaves. The colours are blue, turquoise and purple. Iznik, Turkey, 16th century.

90 A naturalistic spray of carnations, hyacinths and tulips rises from a tuft of leaves. Some of the stems are broken: a quaint device which gives the designer more freedom to arrange the flower heads within the limited space. Iznik, Turkey, 16th century.

91 A flowering prunus tree against a blue background. An element of fantasy is introduced with the large tulips springing from the base of the trunk. Iznik, Turkey, 1570–1600.

92 This design, though featuring flowers like roses and hyacinths painted in their natural colours, has a very pronounced formal and symmetrical composition. Iznik, Turkey, 16th century.

93 In this design which exemplifies the *saz* style vision of the 'enchanted forest' the floral spray motif is now barely recognisable.

94 The extended engraved design from a metal dish-cover. The counter-change feature of the design (in which the shape of the spaces left between the motifs is the same shape as the motif itself) originated in manuscript illuminations which inspired the use of such designs in metalwork and ceramics. *c.* 1600.

95 Tiles painted in blue, green and red. The traditional palmette design uses the counter-change device TOP and CENTRE. Such tiles served as repeat units and made up continuous borders. Iznik, Turkey, 16th century.

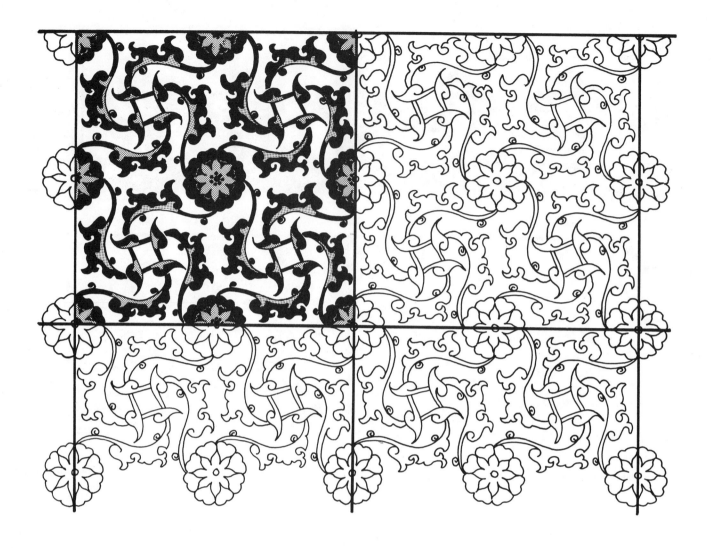

96 TOP Tile painted in blue, turquoise and red on a white ground. Like the tile OPPOSITE it produces an over-all pattern when set with tiles of the same design. The tiles BELOW are mirror images of each other and together make up a repeat unit to produce a continuous border. Iznik, Turkey, 16th century.

97 The designs of the tiles on these pages are elaborations of the traditional split palmette motif in a form also seen in contemporary illuminated manuscripts. Iznik, Turkey, 16th century.

98 Extended engraved designs and borders from an early 16th-century Ottoman brass candlestick.

99 Designs from a candlestick similar to that OPPOSITE. The traditional split palmette scroll design is reserved against a ring-punched ground.

100 This popular motif in Ottoman art is thought to represent the spots and stripes of leopard and tiger skins. Its origins and significance are obscure but the decorative possibilities of this design are illustrated here by a hexagonal tile TOP and border tile BELOW. Damascus, 16th–17th centuries.